Harmony of the Scales

Matthew Petchinsky

Harmony of the Scales

Happy Birthday fellow Libra!

H armony of the Scales: A Libra's Spellcraft for Balance and Beauty
By: Matthew Petchinsky

Introduction to Libra's Influence in Spellcraft

Libra, the seventh sign of the zodiac, is ruled by Venus, the planet of love, beauty, and harmony. This cardinal air sign brings a unique energy into the realm of spellcraft, emphasizing themes of balance, partnership, justice, and the aesthetic nature of existence. Governed by the scales, Libra is all about finding equilibrium in every aspect of life, whether it be relationships, emotions, or the pursuit of fairness. In spellcraft, Libra's influence provides an opportunity to harness these qualities and enhance the caster's innate abilities to bring beauty and harmony into the world.

Libran magic focuses on spells that promote peace, love, reconciliation, justice, and inner balance. Spells inspired by Libra's energy can be seen as intricate dances—gentle yet precise, designed to navigate complex situations with grace. The Libran magical practice often includes a variety of elements that enhance both aesthetic and functional aspects, such as incorporating crystals like rose quartz for love or amethyst for inner peace, as well as utilizing herbs like lavender and rose petals to invoke harmony and calmness.

The Power of Harmony, Beauty, and Relationships in Libran Magic

Libra's deep connection to Venus gifts it with a natural affinity for spells that revolve around beauty and love. In Libran spellcraft, beauty is not limited to physical appearance but extends to the beauty of a harmonious environment, the elegance of well-balanced relationships, and the allure of fairness in justice. Spells performed under Libra's influence often aim to create an atmosphere of serenity and sophistication. Whether you are casting a spell to enhance personal charm, smooth out discord in relationships, or beautify your surroundings, the energy of Libra will amplify your intentions toward harmony and elegance.

Relationships play a central role in Libra's astrological energy. This sign is deeply oriented toward partnership, whether it be romantic, platonic, or even professional. Spells that invoke Libran energy are ideal for enhancing existing bonds, mending misunderstandings, or attracting new, balanced relationships into one's life. Libra's focus on fairness and equality is perfect for spells that seek to establish reciprocity and mutual respect. The key is to bring into alignment the desires and energies of all involved, facilitating communication and compromise.

Justice and fairness are also crucial aspects of Libra's influence. Spells crafted under Libra's watchful eye often revolve around righting wrongs, promoting honesty, and restoring equilibrium to situations where imbalance prevails. This sign is adept at navigating complex dynamics with diplomacy and charm, making its magic particularly potent in spells related to conflict resolution and legal matters. Such spells are infused with the Libran desire for truth and equity, helping to ensure that all parties are treated fairly and with respect.

The Libran Need for Balance and Enhancing Their Natural Gifts Through Spellcraft

The core of Libra's energy is balance. In every area of life, a Libran strives to achieve harmony and equilibrium. When a Libran feels out of sync—whether due to external conflict, internal strife, or an environment that lacks beauty and order—they may experience unease and dissatisfaction. Spellcrafting can serve as a powerful tool for a Libra to restore balance both within themselves and in their surroundings.

Spells that focus on enhancing a Libra's natural gifts—such as their diplomatic skills, artistic abilities, and intuitive understanding of relationships—can lead to profound personal growth. For example, spells for self-love and acceptance help Libra embrace their need for peace and harmony without sacrificing their own desires. Similarly, spells for attracting love and friendship allow Librans to draw balanced and respectful relationships into their lives. These spells work by attuning the caster to the energy of Libra, fostering an environment where their natural qualities can thrive.

Incorporating balance-focused spells into daily practice can aid Libras in navigating life's challenges with greater ease. Rituals involving the balancing of elements, aligning chakras, or setting intentions with scales as a symbolic focal point can reinforce a Libra's connection to equilibrium. Simple practices, like creating charms for inner peace or invoking harmony during mediation spells, can amplify a Libran's ability to handle stress and restore order in chaotic situations.

Harnessing Libra's Influence for Enhanced Spellcraft

When working with Libra's astrological influence, the key is to embrace its dual emphasis on harmony and justice. Every spell cast with Libra's energy should aim to not only fulfill the caster's desires but also maintain the balance of the greater whole. Whether you are performing a love spell, a beauty charm, or a spell for peace in a conflicted relationship, Libra's energy can help guide you toward a balanced outcome.

Libra's love for beauty means that the aesthetic elements of spellcasting take on added significance. The careful arrangement of candles, the use of delicate fragrances, and the thoughtful selection of crystals and herbs can enhance the effectiveness of spells conducted under Libra's sign. Every component of the spell should harmonize to create an atmosphere of serenity and focused intention.

By aligning spellwork with Libra's principles of harmony, beauty, relationships, and justice, you can enhance your magical practice to achieve deeper balance and a greater sense of peace. This introduction serves as a gateway to exploring Libra's enchanting influence in spellcraft, guiding you to create spells that resonate with the Libran quest for equilibrium. As you proceed, remember that true harmony is not the absence of conflict, but the delicate dance of opposites coming together to create something beautiful, just as Libra's scales forever seek to balance the weight of the world.

Chapter 1: Balancing the Scales: A Grounding Spell

Emotional equilibrium is essential for any Libran spellcaster. Libra, ruled by the harmonious planet Venus, constantly seeks to balance the scales in every aspect of life. However, the emotional ups and downs of daily existence can disrupt that inner harmony. This grounding spell is designed to restore emotional equilibrium, using the natural energies of crystals and the phases of the moon to help you center yourself and regain balance. By working with these elements, you can harness the stabilizing power of Libra's energy and maintain a peaceful emotional state, regardless of external circumstances.

The Importance of Emotional Balance for Libra

For Libra, the state of emotional balance is more than just a goal—it's a necessity. When life feels chaotic or emotionally turbulent, Libras can become easily overwhelmed, indecisive, and ungrounded. This grounding spell is designed to help you reconnect with your inner self and find peace amidst the chaos, allowing you to navigate life's challenges with grace and calm. The spell focuses on aligning your emotional energy with the steady, rhythmic cycles of the moon, using crystals to enhance this connection and promote stability.

Understanding the Power of Crystals and Moon Phases

Crystals have long been used in spellcraft for their unique vibrational frequencies and healing properties. In this spell, we will use rose quartz and smoky quartz to channel loving and grounding energies. Rose quartz, known as the "stone of unconditional love," promotes self-love, emotional healing, and calmness. Smoky quartz, with its grounding and stabilizing properties, absorbs negative energy and brings a sense of balance and protection. Together, these crystals create a potent combination that resonates with Libra's desire for harmony and inner peace.

The moon phases provide a natural rhythm that can be harnessed for emotional healing. This spell utilizes the power of the waning moon, a time for release, reflection, and grounding. The waning phase is ideal for letting go of negative emotions, re-centering oneself, and restoring inner harmony. By aligning this spell with the moon's waning energy, you can enhance the grounding effect and promote a deeper sense of emotional equilibrium.

Materials Needed

- A piece of rose quartz (for self-love and emotional healing)
- A piece of smoky quartz (for grounding and protection)
- A small bowl of salt water (for purification and cleansing)
- White candle (for purity and peace)
- A small pouch or cloth (to carry the crystals)
- A notebook or journal (to record intentions and reflections)
- Access to an outdoor space under the night sky (optional, but beneficial)
- A quiet, undisturbed space for meditation

Timing the Spell

Perform this spell during the waning moon, which begins right after the full moon and lasts until the new moon. The waning moon's energy is perfect for releasing negativity and grounding oneself. If possible, select a day when the moon is in an earth sign (Taurus, Virgo, or Capricorn) to amplify the grounding effect. An ideal time to conduct this spell is during the evening, under the moon's gentle light.

Steps for the Grounding Spell
1. Preparing the Sacred Space

Find a quiet space where you can perform the spell without distractions. Cleanse the area by sprinkling salt water in a circle around you, visualizing it creating a protective boundary. Light the white candle, allowing its flame to symbolize purity and peace. Arrange the rose quartz and smoky quartz in front of you. Place the small pouch or cloth nearby, as you will use it to carry the crystals after the spell.

2. Setting Your Intentions

Sit comfortably and close your eyes. Take several deep breaths, inhaling through your nose and exhaling through your mouth. With each breath, imagine inhaling calmness and exhaling tension. Once you feel relaxed, focus your mind on your intention for the spell. Silently state your desire to achieve emotional balance and inner peace.

Say the following affirmation aloud or in your mind:

"By the power of the moon's gentle light, I seek balance and emotional grounding. I release all that disrupts my peace and welcome harmony into my heart."

Repeat this affirmation until you feel connected to its meaning.

3. Connecting with the Crystals

Pick up the rose quartz in your left hand, the hand closest to your heart. Visualize a soft pink light emanating from the crystal, filling you with love, calmness, and healing energy. Feel the crystal's warmth in your palm, radiating a soothing vibration through your body.

Next, pick up the smoky quartz in your right hand, which symbolizes action and protection. Visualize this crystal surrounded by a grounding brown or gray light, anchoring you to the earth. Feel its energy absorb any lingering negativity, bringing stability to your emotions.

Hold both crystals together at your heart center, close your eyes, and breathe deeply. Imagine the energies of both stones intertwining within you, creating a harmonious and balanced energy field.

4. Harnessing the Moon's Energy

If you are outdoors, gaze up at the waning moon. If indoors, close your eyes and visualize the moon's calming, silvery light surrounding you. Envision this light washing over you, gently dissolving any emotional turmoil and restoring your inner harmony.

Imagine the moon's energy flowing into the crystals in your hands, charging them with the power of release and balance. Feel this energy grounding you, rooting you into the earth like a tree with deep, sturdy roots.

5. Grounding and Releasing

Take a deep breath and slowly exhale, imagining any lingering stress, anxiety, or negative emotions leaving your body and being absorbed into the smoky quartz. As you release these emotions, feel the rose quartz filling the space in your heart with love and tranquility.

Visualize the scales of Libra perfectly balanced within you, a symbol of your restored equilibrium. Allow this image to solidify in your mind as you repeat the affirmation:

"With the moon's guidance, I release all that weighs me down. I embrace balance, peace, and harmony."

6. Concluding the Spell

Gently place the crystals into the pouch or cloth. Hold the pouch close to your heart, whispering your gratitude to the moon, the crystals, and the energies of balance. Extinguish the candle, but let its smoke carry your intentions to the universe.

Keep the pouch with you in the coming days, especially when you feel unbalanced or overwhelmed. The crystals will serve as a reminder of your grounding and emotional harmony.

7. Reflecting on Your Experience

After performing the spell, take a few moments to write in your journal. Reflect on how you felt during the spell, any emotions that surfaced, and your overall sense of balance. Writing down your thoughts helps to solidify your intentions and track your progress in maintaining emotional equilibrium.

Final Thoughts

This grounding spell is a powerful tool for restoring emotional balance, a cornerstone of Libra's astrological influence. By using the energies of rose quartz, smoky quartz, and the waning moon, you align yourself with the natural rhythms of the universe, enhancing your ability to navigate life's challenges with grace and calm. Remember, balance is not about avoiding emotions but about learning to flow with them, finding harmony in the ebb and flow.

Perform this spell whenever you feel the scales tipping, whether due to emotional stress, uncertainty, or the chaos of daily life. With each practice, you will deepen your connection to Libra's energy, cultivating a state of emotional equilibrium that resonates throughout your life. In this way, you embody the essence of Libra—poised, harmonious, and ever in pursuit of inner peace.

Chapter 2: The Mirror of Truth: Reflection Spell

In the pursuit of balance and harmony, self-reflection plays a crucial role, especially for a Libra. Libra's quest for equilibrium extends beyond external circumstances; it also includes an inner exploration of the self. However, true self-reflection requires more than just introspection—it requires honesty, acceptance, and the courage to confront one's strengths and weaknesses. This reflection spell, known as "The Mirror of Truth," is designed to help you look inward with clarity and compassion, using the power of a mirror and candlelight to reveal hidden truths and promote self-understanding.

The Importance of Self-Reflection for Libra

Libra, ruled by Venus, seeks harmony in every facet of life, but this can sometimes lead to a tendency to avoid conflict or uncomfortable truths, both internally and externally. By nature, Libras desire to keep the peace, which can result in them masking their true feelings to avoid rocking the boat. However, genuine balance and harmony can only be achieved through the honest acknowledgment of one's thoughts, emotions, desires, and flaws. This spell is designed to illuminate these aspects, allowing a Libran to confront their inner truths and embrace a holistic self-awareness.

Self-reflection helps a Libra reconnect with their inner world, providing insights that guide them toward emotional balance and improved relationships. The Mirror of Truth spell serves as a means of bringing these hidden parts to light, so they can be understood, accepted, and integrated. This spell focuses on using a mirror and candle to tap into one's subconscious, uncovering truths that the conscious mind may have overlooked or suppressed. The soft glow of the candle symbolizes the light of self-awareness, while the mirror acts as a gateway to the soul, reflecting both the known and unknown aspects of one's being.

Materials Needed

- A small hand mirror (dedicated solely for this spell)
- A white candle (for purity and truth)
- Lavender essential oil (for relaxation and mental clarity)
- A clean cloth (to cleanse the mirror)
- A bowl of water mixed with sea salt (for purification)
- A journal or notebook (for recording insights)
- A quiet, dimly lit space where you can sit comfortably

Timing the Spell

This spell is best performed during the waxing gibbous moon phase, which is the period between the first quarter and the full moon. The waxing gibbous is a time of introspection and illumination, ideal for seeking truth and gaining self-awareness. Performing the spell in the evening, when the world is quieter and the mind is more receptive, will enhance its effectiveness.

Steps for the Reflection Spell

1. Preparing the Sacred Space

Choose a quiet, dimly lit area where you will not be disturbed. Before beginning, cleanse your space by sprinkling sea salt water in a circle around you, purifying the energy in the area. Light the white candle and place it on a flat surface in front of you, symbolizing the light of truth and self-awareness.

Prepare the mirror by wiping it down with a clean cloth. As you do so, dab a bit of lavender essential oil onto the cloth, infusing the mirror with calming and clarifying energy. Place the mirror next to the candle, allowing the candlelight to reflect softly onto its surface.

2. Setting Your Intentions

Sit comfortably in front of the mirror, taking several deep breaths to center yourself. With each inhale, draw in peace and clarity; with each exhale, release tension and anxiety. Once you feel relaxed, close your eyes and set your intention for the spell.

Visualize a soft, gentle light surrounding you, enveloping you in a sense of safety and openness. Focus on your desire to see and understand your inner truth. In your mind, affirm your willingness to confront whatever is revealed with compassion and acceptance.

Say the following affirmation aloud or in your mind:

"I seek the truth within myself. With an open heart, I gaze into the mirror, ready to embrace all that I see, for it is through truth that I find balance and harmony."

Repeat this affirmation until you feel it resonate within you, grounding your intention firmly in your consciousness.

3. Connecting with the Mirror

Gaze into the mirror, focusing on the reflection illuminated by the candlelight. As you look, allow your eyes to soften, blurring the details of your physical appearance. Let go of any judgment or self-critique. The goal is not to scrutinize your physical features but to see beyond them into the depths of your inner self.

Continue breathing steadily, allowing your mind to quieten. Gradually, shift your focus from the surface to the eyes—the windows to the soul. In the candle's glow, observe the emotions and thoughts that arise as you stare into your own eyes. You might notice various feelings surfacing: fear, joy, sadness, pride, or even confusion. Allow these emotions to come forth without trying to control them. They are a part of your truth, here to be acknowledged and understood.

4. Invoking Self-Truth

As you continue to gaze into the mirror, speak softly:

"Mirror of truth, reveal to me, all that lies within, so I may see. Shadows and light, love and fear, guide me now, make it clear. With this flame, I seek what's true, to understand myself anew."

Repeat this incantation three times, each time with more conviction. The words serve to invoke the mirror's power, inviting it to reflect the truths hidden within your subconscious.

5. Reflecting and Revealing

After speaking the incantation, return your gaze to your reflection and remain silent. Pay attention to any images, emotions, or thoughts that arise. You may see memories flash across your mind, feel emotions welling up, or hear inner dialogue that you have been ignoring. This is the mirror revealing aspects of yourself that need to be acknowledged.

Do not rush this process; give yourself the time to explore whatever comes up. You may feel a mixture of emotions—some comforting, others challenging. Remember, this is a safe space for self-reflection. Whatever is revealed, accept it as a part of your journey toward self-awareness.

6. Closing the Reflection

When you feel ready to conclude the spell, take a deep breath and close your eyes. Hold the mirror gently in your hands, thanking it for showing you your truth. Whisper words of gratitude for the insights gained, both the pleasant and the difficult.

Say aloud or silently:

"I embrace my truth, whole and clear. With compassion and love, I hold it near. The mirror's reflection, my soul's decree, I accept myself, I choose to be free."

Blow out the candle, signaling the end of the spell. This act releases the energy raised during the ritual and seals your intention for self-understanding.

7. Reflecting on Your Insights

After the spell, immediately write down your thoughts, feelings, and any images or messages you received during the reflection. Journaling is an essential part of this spell, as it allows you to capture fleeting insights and explore them further in the days to come. Note down any surprising revelations, patterns you observed, or emotions that stood out. Reflect on how these truths relate to your current state of mind and circumstances.

Tips for Enhanced Self-Reflection

- **Repeat Monthly:** To deepen your self-understanding, consider performing this spell monthly, ideally during the waxing gibbous moon. Each time, you may uncover different layers of truth, providing ongoing clarity and personal growth.
- **Use Symbolic Objects:** Place a small object (a flower, crystal, or token) next to the mirror to symbolize the aspect of yourself you are focusing on during the spell. For example, use a rose quartz for self-love or an amethyst for inner peace.
- **Incorporate Color:** If you have colored candles, use colors that align with your intentions. White is for purity, but pink can enhance self-love, while blue promotes calmness and truth.

Final Thoughts

The Mirror of Truth spell is a powerful tool for self-reflection, allowing you to confront your inner world with honesty and grace. As a Libra, self-understanding is key to maintaining the balance you seek. By using the mirror and candle to illuminate hidden aspects of your psyche, you open a pathway to deeper self-acceptance and growth. This spell not only reveals the beauty within but also shines light on the shadows, helping you embrace the full spectrum of your being.

Remember, the truths that surface during this spell are not meant to be judged or feared; they are there to guide you toward a more harmonious and balanced existence. Each time you perform the Mirror of Truth spell, you strengthen your ability to face yourself with compassion and integrity, laying the foundation for greater peace and equilibrium in your life.

Chapter 3: Aphrodite's Blessing: Beauty Ritual

In spellcraft, glamour spells are magical rituals designed to enhance one's natural beauty, radiate confidence, and attract positive attention. Among the many deities associated with beauty, love, and charm, Aphrodite stands as the ultimate goddess to invoke for such purposes. Aphrodite, the Greek goddess of love, beauty, and pleasure, embodies the ideals of elegance, allure, and self-love. In this chapter, we delve into "Aphrodite's Blessing," a beauty ritual that calls upon the goddess herself to bestow her blessing upon you, enhancing your natural beauty both inside and out.

This glamour spell is not about changing who you are but instead about magnifying your unique features and qualities. By connecting with Aphrodite's divine energy, you can enhance your natural radiance, boost your self-esteem, and project an irresistible aura of confidence. This spell is ideal for those seeking to feel more attractive, charming, and comfortable in their own skin. It integrates beauty with self-love, empowering you to shine from within.

Understanding the Magic of Glamour and the Role of Aphrodite

Glamour spells are powerful tools in spellcraft that work by altering the way you perceive yourself and the way others perceive you. They don't physically change your features; instead, they create an energetic aura that emphasizes your most attractive qualities. This energy draws others to you, allowing them to see you in a light that reflects the beauty and confidence you project.

Aphrodite, as the goddess of love and beauty, is the perfect deity to call upon for glamour spells. Her influence can fill you with self-assurance and allure, aligning your inner beauty with your outer appearance. Invoking Aphrodite in your ritual opens a channel to her energy, which can help you see and appreciate your own beauty, making you naturally more radiant and magnetic to others.

Materials Needed

- A rose quartz crystal (associated with love and beauty)
- A small bowl of fresh rose petals (symbolizing love and self-care)
- A pink candle (for beauty, love, and attraction)
- A vial of rose water (for purification and anointing)
- A mirror (to reflect Aphrodite's blessing)
- Sea salt (for cleansing)
- Honey (a traditional offering to Aphrodite)
- A shell or a small dish (to hold the honey offering)
- A brush or comb (dedicated solely for this spell)
- A journal or notebook (for recording experiences)

Timing the Ritual

The best time to perform this glamour spell is during a waxing moon, as the moon's growing light symbolizes expansion, attraction, and enhancement. Friday, the day sacred to Venus (Aphrodite's Roman counterpart), is ideal for spells related to beauty, love, and attraction. Early evening, just before dusk, is also an excellent time as it captures the transition from day to night, mirroring the spell's intention to reveal and amplify your beauty.

Steps for the Beauty Ritual

1. Preparing the Sacred Space

Begin by creating a sacred space where you can perform the ritual without disturbances. Cleanse the area with sea salt sprinkled in a circle around you, purifying the space and setting the stage for your spell. Set up the pink candle in front of you and place the rose quartz crystal beside it. Lay out the fresh rose petals in a small bowl and keep the rose water and mirror within reach.

Light the pink candle and take a moment to focus on the soft, glowing flame. This flame represents both Aphrodite's beauty and your own inner radiance that you are about to magnify.

2. Setting Your Intentions

Sit comfortably and hold the rose quartz crystal in your hands. Close your eyes and take several deep breaths, inhaling positivity and exhaling any insecurities or self-doubts. Visualize a soft pink light surrounding you, representing Aphrodite's loving and nurturing energy.

Silently or aloud, set your intention for the ritual. Focus on enhancing your natural beauty, increasing your confidence, and embracing your unique features. Say the following affirmation to invoke Aphrodite's presence:

"Aphrodite, goddess of love and beauty, I call upon you to bless me with your grace. May your radiance illuminate my own, enhancing my natural beauty with love and confidence."

Repeat this affirmation three times, feeling your intention solidify with each repetition.

3. Anointing and Invoking Aphrodite

Dip your fingers into the rose water and anoint your forehead, cheeks, and heart area. As you do this, visualize Aphrodite's energy infusing your being with beauty and self-assurance. Picture her standing beside you, a radiant and ethereal presence, smiling with approval as you honor her with this ritual.

Take the bowl of rose petals and hold it up to the sky or towards the candle, saying:

"Aphrodite, goddess of the rose and sea, accept these petals as a symbol of love and beauty. I offer my gratitude for your presence and seek your blessing to enhance my inner and outer glow."

Place the bowl down and pour a small amount of honey into the shell or dish. Honey is a sacred offering to Aphrodite, symbolizing sweetness, love, and attraction. Place the dish near the candle as a gesture of reverence and respect for the goddess.

4. Gaze into the Mirror

Pick up the mirror and gaze into it, allowing your reflection to become your focal point. As you look at yourself, try to see beyond the physical features to the inner beauty that resides within. Visualize Aphrodite's energy enveloping your reflection, enhancing your allure and amplifying your confidence.

With the rose quartz still in your hand, say the following incantation:

"Mirror of truth, reflection of light, show me the beauty both within and outside. Aphrodite's grace, upon me now fall, enhancing my charm, captivating all."

As you speak, imagine your reflection glowing with a soft, pink aura, radiating love, beauty, and self-assurance. Picture this light emanating from you, filling the room and extending out into the world.

5. The Glamour Ritual

Take the brush or comb and begin to brush your hair gently. As you do so, visualize Aphrodite's energy flowing through the brush, coating each strand with her blessing. If you prefer, you can stroke your hands over your skin in the same way, imagining the goddess's touch enhancing your natural beauty.

With each stroke, affirm:

"Aphrodite's grace in every strand, beauty and charm at my command."

Repeat this motion slowly and deliberately, focusing on the intention of enhancing your natural beauty and radiance. Continue until you feel a surge of confidence and self-love building within you.

6. Sealing the Spell

To seal the spell, take the rose quartz and hold it close to your heart. Close your eyes and envision the pink aura from the mirror infusing the crystal with Aphrodite's energy. This crystal will serve as a charm that carries the spell's power with you, enhancing your beauty and confidence wherever you go.

Say the following words:

"By Aphrodite's blessing, my beauty shines bright, inside and out, by day and night. I seal this spell with love and grace; my radiance now takes its place."

Blow out the candle, allowing the smoke to carry your intention to the universe. Take a moment to thank Aphrodite for her presence and blessing, feeling gratitude for the newfound beauty and confidence that you have embraced.

7. Reflect and Carry the Energy

After completing the ritual, write down your experience in your journal. Reflect on how you felt during the spell and any insights that arose. Note the sensations, emotions, and visualizations you encountered while invoking Aphrodite.

Carry the rose quartz crystal with you or place it on your vanity as a reminder of the goddess's blessing and your inner beauty. Whenever you feel self-doubt creeping in, hold the crystal and reconnect with the energy of the spell, reaffirming your beauty and worth.

Tips for Enhancing the Glamour Spell

- **Regular Practice:** Perform this spell whenever you feel the need for a boost in self-confidence or wish to project an enhanced sense of beauty. Repeating the ritual regularly strengthens its effect and deepens your connection with Aphrodite's energy.
- **Use Other Aphrodisiac Scents:** To amplify the spell, you can add other beauty-enhancing elements, such as jasmine or rose incense, which are sacred to Aphrodite.
- **Carry the Rose Quartz:** Keep the rose quartz in your purse, pocket, or makeup bag as a talisman. Whenever you touch it, recall the spell and its affirmation to reignite your inner and outer radiance.

Final Thoughts

"Aphrodite's Blessing" is a potent glamour spell that works by harmonizing your inner and outer beauty, creating a magnetic aura that draws positive attention. By invoking the goddess Aphrodite, you invite her loving and enchanting energy into your life, enhancing your self-esteem and revealing your natural allure to the world. This ritual is more than a superficial beauty spell; it's an affirmation of self-love and self-appreciation, empowering you to embrace your unique charm with grace and confidence.

As a Libra, beauty and harmony are integral to your sense of self. By performing this ritual, you align with your zodiac's ruling energy, magnifying your natural elegance and charm. Remember, true beauty is a reflection of inner balance and self-love. With Aphrodite's blessing, you not only enhance your outward appearance but also nurture the radiant spirit that resides within.

Chapter 4: Weighing the Heart: Feather-Light Mind Spell

Mental clarity and peace of mind are invaluable treasures, especially for a Libra, who is naturally inclined to overthink and strive for balance in every situation. However, the constant weighing of options, concern for fairness, and desire to maintain harmony can sometimes become overwhelming, leading to mental fatigue and emotional burden. "Weighing the Heart: Feather-Light Mind Spell" is designed to help you release these mental burdens and achieve a state of clarity and tranquility. This spell draws inspiration from the ancient Egyptian concept of the heart's weighing against the feather of Ma'at, the goddess of truth, balance, and order. In this spell, you will use the symbolic power of a feather to lighten your mental load and restore peace to your mind.

The feather-light mind spell is intended to unburden your thoughts, alleviate anxiety, and promote a sense of mental clarity. It uses simple yet potent components, such as a feather, a white candle, and soothing herbs, to invoke the energies of Ma'at, goddess of balance, and Libra's harmonious nature. By focusing on the lightness of the feather, you can release the heaviness of stress, overthinking, and doubt, allowing for a more peaceful and balanced state of mind.

Understanding the Importance of Mental Clarity for Libra

Libras are natural diplomats, always striving to maintain equilibrium in their personal lives, relationships, and inner thoughts. This inclination can often result in a cluttered and overloaded mind. Thoughts race back and forth, weighing every possible outcome in the quest for the "right" decision. When overwhelmed by these mental burdens, a Libra's sense of balance is disrupted, leading to anxiety, indecision, and emotional distress.

By performing the Feather-Light Mind Spell, you can invoke the energy of Ma'at and the balance-seeking nature of Libra to cleanse your mind of clutter, release unnecessary worries, and achieve a state of mental serenity. This spell is not just about clearing the mind but also about embracing the natural ebb and flow of thoughts with the lightness and grace of a feather.

Materials Needed

- A white feather (symbolizing lightness, clarity, and peace)
- A white candle (representing purity, clarity, and illumination)
- A small bowl of dried lavender or chamomile (to calm the mind)
- A pinch of sea salt (for purification)
- A small piece of paper and a pen
- A fireproof bowl or dish (for burning paper safely)
- A bowl of water (for cleansing)
- A quiet, comfortable space to perform the spell
- A journal or notebook (for recording reflections)

Timing the Spell

This spell is most effective when performed during the waning moon phase, as this is a time of release and letting go. The waning moon's energy supports the removal of mental burdens, negative thoughts, and anxieties. Performing the spell in the evening, when the mind naturally seeks rest and calm, can enhance its effectiveness.

Steps for the Feather-Light Mind Spell

1. Preparing the Sacred Space

Begin by creating a peaceful, quiet space where you can perform the spell without disturbances. Arrange your items in front of you: the white candle, feather, bowl of dried lavender or chamomile, sea salt, paper, pen, and fireproof bowl. Light the candle, placing it in the center of your space to symbolize clarity and illumination. The candle's flame will serve as a beacon to dispel the fog of confusion and illuminate the path to a lighter mind.

Sprinkle a small pinch of sea salt around your area to cleanse the space and invite pure, balanced energy. Set the bowl of water nearby; you will use it for cleansing at the end of the ritual.

2. Setting Your Intentions

Sit comfortably and close your eyes. Take several deep breaths, inhaling calmness and exhaling tension. Visualize a warm, golden light surrounding you, bringing a sense of peace and clarity. Hold the feather gently in your hand and focus on its lightness. This feather will symbolize the mental state you are aiming to achieve—light, clear, and free of heavy burdens.

Silently or aloud, set your intention for the spell. Focus on the mental burdens you wish to release, whether they are worries, anxieties, indecision, or overthinking. Say the following affirmation to invoke the lightness of mind you desire:

"By the power of Ma'at and the grace of balance, I release all that weighs heavy on my mind. May my thoughts be light as a feather, my heart clear and at peace."

Repeat this affirmation until you feel your intention firmly rooted in your consciousness.

3. Writing Down Your Burdens

Take the piece of paper and pen. Write down the thoughts, worries, or mental burdens that have been weighing you down. Be as specific or general as you need to be—this is a sacred space where you can freely express what has been clouding your mind. Each word you write represents a piece of mental weight that you will soon release.

Once you have finished writing, hold the paper in both hands and take a deep breath. Visualize each burden being absorbed into the paper, ready to be transformed and released.

4. Invoking the Lightness of the Feather

Hold the feather above the piece of paper and say:

"Feather of light, guide my thoughts. As you float upon the air, so too shall my worries disperse, leaving my mind clear and my heart at peace."

Wave the feather gently over the paper, as if brushing away the heaviness of your thoughts. Visualize the feather's lightness transferring to your mind, lifting the weight of your burdens.

5. Burning and Releasing the Burdens

Place the piece of paper into the fireproof bowl. Using the candle's flame, carefully light the paper on fire. As it burns, visualize your worries, anxieties, and mental clutter turning to smoke and dissipating into the air. Watch as the flame consumes the paper, transforming your burdens into lightness and clarity.

While the paper burns, say:

"By fire's light and feather's grace, my burdens now burn and leave no trace. With Ma'at's blessing, my mind is clear, light as a feather, free from fear."

Allow the paper to burn completely. As the flame dies out, imagine all your mental burdens vanishing, replaced by a sense of calm and peace.

6. Cleansing and Sealing the Spell

Take the bowl of water and dip your fingers into it. Gently sprinkle the water over the feather, symbolizing a final cleansing of your mind and sealing of the spell's energy. Then, lightly brush the feather across your forehead, affirming the clarity and lightness you have invoked.

Say the closing affirmation:

"With this feather's lightness, I am free. My mind is clear; peace resides in me."

Extinguish the candle, letting its smoke carry your intentions to the universe. Feel the calmness settle within you as the ritual comes to an end.

7. Reflecting on the Experience

After completing the spell, take a moment to sit quietly and observe how you feel. Notice any sensations of lightness, calm, or mental clarity. When ready, write down your thoughts and experiences in your journal. Reflect on the worries you released and how you intend to maintain this sense of peace in the coming days.

Tips for Enhancing Mental Clarity

- **Use the Feather as a Talisman:** Keep the feather in a safe place, such as on your bedside table or in a journal, as a reminder of your intention to maintain a clear and light mind. Whenever you feel mental burdens returning, hold the feather and reconnect with the energy of the spell.
- **Incorporate Soothing Scents:** If desired, use lavender or chamomile incense during the ritual to promote relaxation and mental clarity. The scent of these herbs can help calm the mind and enhance the spell's effects.
- **Practice Regularly:** This spell can be performed whenever you feel overwhelmed or mentally burdened. The more you practice, the stronger your connection to the spell's energy and the easier it will become to release mental clutter.

Final Thoughts

"Weighing the Heart: Feather-Light Mind Spell" is a powerful way to release mental burdens and promote clarity and peace. Inspired by the ancient wisdom of Ma'at and the feather's lightness, this spell allows you to free your mind from the weight of worries, doubts, and overthinking. By aligning with the balanced and harmonious nature of Libra, you create an inner environment where calmness and clear thinking can flourish.

This spell is not about ignoring challenges or avoiding difficult thoughts but rather about letting go of the mental heaviness that prevents you from achieving balance and peace. By releasing these burdens, you open up space for new perspectives, ideas, and insights to arise. Use this ritual as a tool to reconnect with your inner sense of harmony and to remind yourself that, like the feather, your mind can float above life's complexities with grace and ease.

Chapter 5: Venusian Charm: Attraction Spell

Attracting love, friendship, and harmonious relationships is at the heart of Libran energy, guided by Venus, the planet of love, beauty, and connection. Venus' influence grants Libra a natural magnetism, making them skilled in cultivating warm and inviting connections. However, there are times when even a Libra may need an extra boost to attract the love or friendships they seek. The "Venusian Charm: Attraction Spell" is designed to channel Venus's loving energy using rose petals and honey, two symbols of sweetness and romance, to draw love and friendship into your life.

This attraction spell works by amplifying your natural charm, enhancing your aura, and inviting others to be drawn to your warmth and loving nature. It is not meant to manipulate or force relationships but rather to align your energy with the qualities that naturally attract love and friendships. By invoking the powers of Venus and using ingredients that symbolize affection and sweetness, you will radiate an inviting aura that encourages connections with others who resonate with your desires for love, friendship, and harmony.

The Power of Rose Petals and Honey in Venusian Magic

In Venusian magic, roses and honey hold significant symbolic power. Roses, especially pink and red varieties, have long been associated with love, romance, and beauty. Their petals embody the gentleness and warmth of love, making them a powerful tool in spells designed to attract affection and friendship. Honey, on the other hand, represents sweetness, attraction, and the nectar of life. Its sticky, golden texture symbolizes the allure that draws people together and the sweetness of relationships.

By incorporating rose petals and honey into this spell, you create a potent blend of Venusian energy that enhances your personal magnetism and makes you more receptive to love and friendship. The spell acts like a charm, infusing you with the irresistible qualities that Venus embodies: beauty, grace, and loving energy.

Materials Needed

- Fresh or dried rose petals (preferably pink or red for love and friendship)
- A small jar of honey (for sweetness and attraction)
- A pink candle (to represent Venus's loving energy)
- A piece of rose quartz (for love and harmony)
- A small piece of parchment or paper
- A red or pink pen
- A bowl of water mixed with sea salt (for cleansing)
- A sachet or pouch (to carry the spell's charm)
- A quiet, comfortable space for the spell
- A journal or notebook (for recording reflections)

Timing the Spell

The ideal time to perform this spell is on a Friday, the day ruled by Venus, which governs love, beauty, and attraction. To enhance the spell's power, perform it during a waxing or full moon, when the moon's energy supports growth, attraction, and manifestation. Early evening is a suitable time, as the transitional period between day and night resonates with the spell's intent to invite new connections into your life.

Steps for the Attraction Spell

1. Preparing the Sacred Space

Find a quiet, comfortable space where you will not be disturbed. Begin by cleansing the area with the sea salt water to purify the energy around you, preparing it for the spell. Light the pink candle and place it in front of you to symbolize the loving energy of Venus. Set the rose petals, honey, parchment, pen, rose quartz, and pouch nearby, within easy reach.

Take a moment to center yourself by taking several deep breaths. Inhale deeply, envisioning yourself drawing in the loving and magnetic energy of Venus. Exhale slowly, releasing any self-doubt or negativity that may hinder your ability to attract love and friendships.

2. Setting Your Intentions

Hold the rose quartz in your hand and close your eyes. Visualize a soft pink light emanating from the stone, surrounding you with the warm, loving energy of Venus. Feel this energy fill your heart, expanding outward to create an aura of attraction and warmth around you.

Focus your mind on what you seek to attract—whether it is romantic love, deep friendship, or simply more warmth and connection in your social circle. Be specific yet open, allowing the universe to bring the best possible relationships into your life.

Silently or aloud, state your intention for the spell. For example:

"With the blessing of Venus, goddess of love and beauty, I open my heart to attract love, friendship, and harmony. May my aura radiate warmth, drawing to me those who align with my desires and spirit."

Repeat this affirmation until you feel it resonate within your being, solidifying your intention.

3. Writing Your Desires

Take the parchment or paper and the red or pink pen. Write down the qualities you wish to attract in your relationships, whether it's love, friendship, or both. For example, you might write: "I attract loving, supportive, and joyful friendships" or "I open myself to a romantic relationship filled with love, respect, and harmony." Be clear and honest about what you seek.

Once you have written your desires, fold the paper and hold it to your heart. Visualize these words glowing with a pink light, radiating the energy of attraction and love.

4. Anointing with Honey and Rose Petals

Place the folded paper in front of the pink candle. Pour a small amount of honey over the paper, symbolizing the sweetness you wish to draw into your life. As you do this, imagine your heart radiating warmth and light, attracting love and friendship like honey attracts bees.

Take a handful of rose petals and sprinkle them over the honey-covered paper. As you sprinkle the petals, say:

"Sweet as honey, soft as rose, love and friendship now unclose. Venus, goddess, hear my plea; bring warmth and joy, so mote it be."

Visualize the honey and rose petals shimmering with a gentle, pink glow, drawing in the energies of love and harmony toward you.

5. Creating the Charm Pouch

Carefully gather the paper, honey, and rose petals together and place them into the sachet or pouch. Add the rose quartz crystal to the pouch, infusing it with loving energy. Hold the pouch in your hands and close your eyes. Focus on the warmth and sweetness of the spell's energy, feeling it resonate within you.

Whisper to the pouch:

"By Venus's charm, I now attract love and friendship, strong and intact. With this pouch, my wishes take flight; love and harmony, come to light."

Visualize the pouch glowing softly, empowered by the energy of Venus and your intention.

6. Sealing the Spell

Seal the pouch and hold it over the flame of the pink candle (taking care not to let it catch fire) to absorb the candle's loving light. Then, extinguish the candle, letting the smoke carry your intention to the universe.

Say the following words to seal the spell:

"As I will, so mote it be. Love and friendship, now come to me."

Carry the pouch with you as a charm, keeping it in your bag, pocket, or under your pillow to maintain the spell's influence.

7. Reflecting on the Experience

After completing the spell, sit quietly and take a few moments to reflect on how you feel. Notice any warmth, calmness, or sense of openness that may have arisen during the ritual. When ready, write down your experience in your journal, noting any insights, sensations, or emotions that surfaced. This reflection helps reinforce your intention and keeps you aligned with the energy of attraction.

Tips for Enhancing the Attraction Spell

- **Recharge the Charm:** To keep the spell's energy active, recharge the pouch by placing it under the light of the waxing or full moon or by holding it over a pink candle on Fridays.
- **Use Scent:** If desired, you can anoint the pouch with a few drops of rose or jasmine oil to enhance its Venusian charm and amplify the aura of attraction.
- **Visualize Daily:** Whenever you hold the pouch, close your eyes and visualize the qualities you wish to attract, reaffirming your intention. This keeps the energy of the spell vibrant and focused.

Final Thoughts

The "Venusian Charm: Attraction Spell" is a beautiful way to channel the loving, harmonious energy of Venus to attract love and friendships. By using rose petals and honey, you harness the natural symbols of sweetness, affection, and connection, allowing you to radiate an aura of warmth and charm that draws others to you.

Remember, this spell is not about forcing relationships but rather about aligning your energy with the qualities you seek in others. It opens your heart to love and friendship, enhancing your natural magnetism and inviting those who resonate with your desires into your life. As a Libra, this spell resonates deeply with your love for harmony, beauty, and meaningful connections. By invoking Venus's blessing, you empower yourself to create a loving and supportive network of relationships that enrich your life.

Chapter 6: Harmonious Union: Relationship Balance Spell

For a Libra, harmony in relationships is paramount. Governed by Venus, the planet of love, Libra seeks connections that embody balance, mutual respect, and fairness. However, even the most harmonious relationships can encounter moments of tension, misunderstanding, or imbalance. When these disruptions occur, they can weigh heavily on a Libra's heart, disrupting their sense of peace and equilibrium. The "Harmonious Union: Relationship Balance Spell" is designed to restore harmony and tranquility in relationships, using the calming properties of herbs and crystals to ease conflict, promote understanding, and foster a balanced union.

This ritual aims to create a calming environment where differences can be resolved, communication can flow freely, and love can flourish once again. By incorporating specific herbs and crystals known for their soothing and harmonizing energies, this spell works to heal rifts, strengthen bonds, and re-establish a sense of equilibrium in relationships. It can be used for romantic partners, friendships, family dynamics, or any relationship that requires restoration and balance.

The Power of Herbs and Crystals in Relationship Spells

Herbs and crystals have been utilized in spellcraft for centuries due to their natural energies and vibrational properties. In this spell, you will use herbs like lavender, chamomile, and rosemary to invoke peace, understanding, and mental clarity—qualities essential for resolving conflicts and restoring harmony. Lavender is renowned for its calming effects, easing tensions and promoting a peaceful atmosphere. Chamomile, a symbol of peace and relaxation, helps soothe emotional turmoil, while rosemary encourages clarity, respect, and clear communication.

Crystals such as rose quartz and amethyst amplify these calming effects. Rose quartz, often called the "stone of love," opens the heart to compassion, forgiveness, and unconditional love. Amethyst, with its tranquil energy, helps dissolve negativity and promotes emotional balance. By combining these herbs and crystals in a ritual, you create a powerful blend of energies that support the healing and harmonizing of relationships.

Materials Needed

- Dried lavender (for calmness and emotional healing)
- Dried chamomile (for peace and relaxation)
- Dried rosemary (for clarity and mutual respect)
- Rose quartz crystal (for love and harmony)
- Amethyst crystal (for emotional balance and tranquility)
- A pink or white candle (to symbolize love and peace)
- A small bowl of water mixed with sea salt (for purification)
- A small cloth bag or pouch (to create a charm)
- A piece of parchment or paper and a pen
- A fireproof bowl (for burning intentions)
- A quiet, comfortable space for the ritual
- A journal or notebook (to record your reflections)

Timing the Ritual

This spell is most effective when performed during a waxing or full moon, as these phases symbolize growth, renewal, and illumination. The waxing moon's energy supports the strengthening of relationships and the restoration of harmony, while the full moon brings clarity and the culmination of emotional intentions. Ideally, perform this ritual on a Friday, the day ruled by Venus, to amplify the loving and harmonizing energies of the spell.

Steps for the Relationship Balance Spell

1. Preparing the Sacred Space

Choose a quiet, comfortable space where you can perform the ritual without disturbances. Cleanse the area by sprinkling sea salt water in a circle around you to purify the space and invite balanced energy. Set up the pink or white candle in front of you, along with the dried herbs, crystals, parchment, pen, cloth bag, and fireproof bowl.

Light the candle to symbolize the intention of restoring peace, love, and harmony within your relationship. Take a moment to focus on the flame, allowing it to calm your mind and center your thoughts.

2. Setting Your Intentions

Sit comfortably and close your eyes. Take several deep breaths, inhaling calmness and exhaling tension. Hold the rose quartz in your left hand (the receiving hand) and the amethyst in your right hand (the projecting hand). Visualize a soft pink light radiating from the rose quartz, filling your heart with love and compassion. Then, envision a soothing purple light from the amethyst enveloping your mind, bringing emotional balance and clarity.

Focus on the relationship you wish to heal or balance. Visualize you and the other person surrounded by the pink and purple lights, gently dissolving any tension or discord between you. Set your intention for the spell by saying the following affirmation:

"With the power of love and balance, I seek harmony in our connection. May peace replace conflict, may love replace doubt, and may understanding flow between us."

Repeat this affirmation until you feel your intention resonating deeply within your heart.

3. Writing and Releasing Intentions

Take the parchment or paper and pen. Write down the aspects of the relationship that you wish to heal, balance, or strengthen. Be specific but gentle in your wording. For example, you might write: "I release our misunderstandings and welcome open, loving communication" or "I seek peace and mutual respect between us." This step is about acknowledging the current imbalances while inviting positive change.

Once you have written your intentions, fold the paper and hold it over the candle's flame (taking care not to let it catch fire). Allow the warmth of the candle to infuse the paper with the energy of love and harmony.

4. Burning the Intentions

Place the folded paper into the fireproof bowl. Light it with the candle flame and watch as it burns. As the paper turns to ash, visualize the negative energies or conflicts in the relationship being consumed by the fire and transformed into light and peace.

As the paper burns, say:

"By fire's light, I release the pain. Balance and harmony shall remain. With this flame, all discord ends, love and peace, to us I send."

Allow the paper to burn completely, then gently scatter the ashes into the bowl of water mixed with sea salt. This represents the final cleansing of the relationship's energies.

5. Creating the Herbal and Crystal Charm

Take the cloth bag and begin adding the herbs one by one, starting with lavender. As you add each herb, focus on its properties:

- **Lavender:** Sprinkle into the bag while saying, *"Lavender, bring calm and peace, soothe our hearts and let tensions cease."*
- **Chamomile:** Add to the bag while saying, *"Chamomile, gentle and mild, bring relaxation, peace, and reconcile."*
- **Rosemary:** Add to the bag while saying, *"Rosemary, clear and true, restore respect between us two."*

Next, add the rose quartz and amethyst crystals to the bag. Visualize these crystals radiating love and balance, amplifying the energy of the herbs.

Hold the bag close to your heart and say:

"With herbs and stones, our bond I mend, love and harmony I now send. By Venus's grace, balance is found, peace and love, in us abound."

Picture the bag glowing with a warm, soothing light, filled with the intention of harmony and balance.

6. Sealing the Spell

Seal the bag and place it next to the candle. Allow the candle to burn down naturally if possible, letting its light continue to infuse the charm with peaceful energy. If you need to extinguish it sooner, snuff it out (do not blow) to preserve the intention.

Hold the charm in your hands and whisper:

"As this spell is cast, may balance last. By the love of Venus, harmony is restored. So mote it be."

Keep the charm in a safe place, such as under your pillow or in a drawer where you store personal items, to continuously radiate its harmonizing energy into your relationship.

7. Reflecting on the Ritual

After the ritual, sit quietly and reflect on how you feel. Notice any sense of relief, calmness, or renewed hope for the relationship. Write down your experience in your journal, including the intentions you set and any insights that surfaced during the spell. This reflection helps anchor your intentions and align your thoughts with the spell's energy.

Tips for Maintaining Relationship Harmony

- **Recharge the Charm:** To keep the spell's influence strong, recharge the herbal and crystal charm by holding it over a pink or white candle on Fridays or during the full moon.
- **Use Regularly:** This spell can be performed whenever you feel tension or imbalance in a relationship. Regular practice helps maintain a sense of peace and balance.
- **Incorporate Daily Affirmations:** Whenever you feel a conflict arising, hold the charm and recite the affirmation, "I welcome harmony and balance into our relationship," to reinforce the spell's energy.

Final Thoughts

The "Harmonious Union: Relationship Balance Spell" is a beautiful and powerful ritual designed to restore peace, love, and understanding in relationships. By combining the calming properties of herbs and the harmonizing energies of crystals, you create a soothing and supportive environment for healing and reconciliation.

This spell aligns with Libra's natural inclination towards balance and fairness, offering a pathway to dissolve conflict, enhance communication, and strengthen bonds. Remember, this ritual is not about forcing outcomes but rather about opening your heart to love and mutual respect. By invoking the energies of Venus, you embrace the principles of harmony and compassion, inviting them to flow freely within your relationships. With each performance of this spell, you nurture the loving connections in your life, reinforcing the balance that brings peace and joy to your heart.

Chapter 7: Scales of Justice: Truth Revelation Spell

Libras, governed by Venus, embody a natural desire for harmony and fairness. However, achieving true balance in life requires honesty and transparency, not just from oneself but also from others. When truths are obscured or secrets lie hidden, it can disturb the peace and equilibrium that Libras seek. The "Scales of Justice: Truth Revelation Spell" is designed to uncover hidden truths in situations, whether they involve interpersonal relationships, personal dilemmas, or uncertain circumstances. By using a mix of truth-promoting herbs, this spell calls upon the energies of fairness and justice to illuminate what has been concealed, ensuring clarity and honesty prevail.

This spell works by aligning you with the vibrational frequency of truth. It draws on the power of herbs that have been historically associated with truth-seeking, clarity, and mental fortitude. Through the spell's practice, you invoke the universe's energy to bring hidden truths to light, allowing you to weigh the scales of justice and make informed, balanced decisions.

The Power of Truth-Promoting Herbs

Certain herbs possess energetic properties that align with truth, clarity, and mental sharpness. In this spell, we use bay leaves, sage, thyme, and rosemary to create a powerful blend that opens the mind, promotes honesty, and clears away deceitful energy. Bay leaves are renowned for their ability to enhance intuition and reveal hidden information. Sage purifies the mind, removing the fog of confusion and deceit. Thyme is linked to courage and mental clarity, enabling one to face the truth, while rosemary sharpens the mind, encouraging clear thinking and awareness. Combined, these herbs create an energetic field that encourages truth to surface.

Materials Needed

- Dried bay leaves (for intuition and revealing hidden information)
- Dried sage (for purification and clearing deceit)
- Dried thyme (for mental clarity and courage)

- Dried rosemary (for sharpness of mind)
- A small black or blue candle (to symbolize truth and revelation)
- A piece of parchment or paper and a pen
- A fireproof bowl (for burning herbs)
- A small bowl of water mixed with sea salt (for cleansing)
- A cloth pouch or small jar (to store the herbal mix)
- A quiet, comfortable space for the ritual
- A journal or notebook (to record your findings)

Timing the Spell

This spell is best performed during a waxing moon phase when the moon's energy supports growth, revelation, and illumination. Ideally, perform it on a Wednesday, the day ruled by Mercury, which governs communication, intellect, and truth-seeking. Evening is an ideal time, as the setting sun signifies the transition from light to shadow, mirroring the unveiling of hidden truths.

Steps for the Truth Revelation Spell

1. Preparing the Sacred Space

Begin by selecting a quiet, comfortable area where you will not be disturbed. Cleanse the space by sprinkling sea salt water around you, purifying the environment to invite clarity and honesty. Set up the black or blue candle in front of you, representing the light of truth that will penetrate the darkness of deceit. Place the dried herbs, parchment, pen, fireproof bowl, and pouch within easy reach.

Light the candle, focusing on its flame as a beacon of truth and illumination. The candle will serve as the focal point of the ritual, symbolizing your intention to uncover the truths that are hidden.

2. Setting Your Intentions

Sit comfortably and close your eyes. Take several deep breaths, inhaling clarity and exhaling confusion or fear. In your mind, visualize a set of scales slowly tipping until they become perfectly balanced. This symbolizes the harmony and fairness you wish to achieve by uncovering the truth.

Hold the intention in your mind to uncover hidden truths in a specific situation. Be as clear as possible about what you seek to reveal. You might focus on a relationship, a personal question, or a situation clouded by uncertainty. Say the following affirmation to set your intention:

"By the power of truth and balance, I seek what lies concealed. Let the veil be lifted, and hidden truths revealed. With clarity and fairness, let justice be done."

Repeat this affirmation until you feel it resonate within your mind and heart, aligning you with the spell's purpose.

3. Writing Your Question or Situation

Take the piece of parchment and pen. Write down the question, situation, or area of your life where you seek clarity and truth. Be specific in your wording, as this will focus the spell's energy on the area where truth needs to be uncovered.

Once you have written it down, hold the parchment over the candle's flame (carefully, without letting it catch fire) to infuse it with the energy of truth. Visualize the flame burning away any lies, illusions, or confusion surrounding the matter.

4. Creating the Herbal Blend

Place the fireproof bowl in front of you and begin adding the herbs one by one:

- **Bay Leaves:** Crush a few bay leaves into the bowl, saying, *"Bay leaf, reveal what's hidden, show me truth, by none forbidden."*
- **Sage:** Add the dried sage to the bowl, saying, *"Sage, purify the mind and clear away deceit. Reveal the truth, bold and complete."*
- **Thyme:** Add the thyme while saying, *"Thyme, give me courage to face what's true, mental clarity to see through."*
- **Rosemary:** Add the rosemary to the bowl, saying, *"Rosemary, sharpen my sight, uncover what's buried, bring it to light."*

As you add each herb, visualize it radiating a light that grows brighter with each addition, forming a circle of clarity and truth around you.

5. Burning the Herbal Blend

Place the parchment with your question or situation into the fire-proof bowl on top of the herbs. Carefully light the parchment with the candle flame, allowing it to ignite the herbs beneath. As the herbs and parchment burn, visualize the smoke rising as a signal to the universe, carrying your intention for truth and clarity.

While the herbs burn, recite the incantation:

"By herbs of truth and flame of night, reveal what's hidden, bring it to light. By scales of justice, balanced and fair, let the truth be known, laid bare."

Watch as the smoke rises, carrying your request for truth to the universe. Trust that as the smoke dissipates, so too will the veils of illusion, allowing clarity and truth to enter your life.

6. Creating the Truth Charm

After the herbs and parchment have burned completely, allow the ashes to cool. Gather the ashes and place them into the cloth pouch or small jar. This will become your truth charm, infused with the energy of the herbs and your intention.

Hold the pouch close to your heart and say:

"With this charm, truth I hold. By flame and herb, secrets unfold. As I carry this token near, hidden truths shall now appear."

Visualize the charm glowing with a subtle blue or white light, radiating an aura of truth-seeking energy. Keep this charm with you, especially when you are dealing with situations where truth and clarity are needed.

7. Sealing the Spell

To seal the spell, blow out the candle, allowing the smoke to rise as a final signal to the universe of your intention. As you do so, say:

"Truth be revealed, as the scales decree. By justice and balance, so mote it be."

Place the charm in your pocket, purse, or another safe place where it can remain close to you. It will continue to work on your behalf, aligning you with the truth and illuminating hidden aspects of the situation.

8. Reflecting on the Ritual

After completing the spell, sit quietly and observe any sensations, emotions, or thoughts that arise. Pay attention to any insights or intuitive nudges that may surface. Write down your experience in your journal, including the question or situation you focused on, your feelings during the spell, and any immediate realizations or shifts in perception.

Tips for Enhancing Truth Revelation

- **Recharge the Charm:** To keep the charm's energy active, recharge it by placing it under the light of a waxing moon or by holding it over a black or blue candle.
- **Use Regularly:** This spell can be performed whenever you feel the need for truth to come to light, whether in relationships, work, or personal introspection.
- **Incorporate Meditation.** Carry the truth charm with you during meditation to enhance your ability to receive insights and revelations.

Final Thoughts

The "Scales of Justice: Truth Revelation Spell" is a powerful ritual for uncovering hidden truths and achieving mental and emotional clarity. By working with the energies of herbs known for their truth-promoting properties and focusing on your intention for fairness and honesty, you align yourself with the vibrational frequency of truth.

This spell reflects Libra's innate desire for balance, fairness, and transparency, ensuring that the scales of justice tip in favor of clarity and truth. It is not about forcing revelations but about creating a space where truth can naturally surface, free from the shadows of deception and confusion. With each performance of this spell, you strengthen your connection to honesty, justice, and balance, allowing you to navigate life's complexities with the light of truth as your guide.

Chapter 8: The Birthday Spell: A Celebration of Self

A birthday marks the beginning of a new personal year, an ideal moment to reflect on past achievements, release what no longer serves you, and set intentions for the future. For Libras, whose energy revolves around balance, harmony, beauty, and self-improvement, a birthday is the perfect time to align with their ruling elements and embrace the path to personal growth. "The Birthday Spell: A Celebration of Self" is a ritual designed to harness the power of this special day to create a clear vision for the year ahead.

This spell calls upon Libra's ruling elements—air and Venusian energy—to set intentions that promote balance, harmony, and personal development. By working with candles, symbols of illumination and transformation, and incorporating Libra's elements, you channel your desires into the universe, creating a roadmap for the year to come. This ritual not only celebrates your journey but also empowers you to manifest your highest aspirations.

Understanding Libra's Ruling Elements in the Birthday Spell

Libra is an air sign ruled by Venus, the planet of love, beauty, and harmony. Air represents intellect, communication, clarity, and the movement of ideas, which are key to a Libra's ability to connect, deliberate, and seek balance. Venusian energy embodies love, beauty, attraction, and the pursuit of harmonious relationships and environments.

In this birthday spell, you will use these elements to illuminate your path for the year ahead. Air is symbolized by incense, representing the clarity and inspiration needed to define your goals, while candles signify the light of Venus, infusing your intentions with warmth, beauty, and love. Together, they create a powerful combination that helps you celebrate your past, embrace your present, and step boldly into your future.

Materials Needed

- Three candles: one pink (Venus and love), one blue (air and clarity), and one white (purity and new beginnings)
- Rose petals (symbolizing beauty, love, and the Venusian energy of Libra)
- A small bowl of dried lavender (for calmness and self-love)
- Incense (sandalwood, frankincense, or lavender) to represent the element of air
- A piece of parchment or paper and a pen
- A small mirror (to reflect self-love and intentions)
- A small bowl of water mixed with sea salt (for purification)
- A cloth pouch or envelope (to hold your written intentions)
- A quiet, comfortable space for the ritual
- A journal or notebook (to record your reflections)

Timing the Spell

This spell is best performed on your birthday, a day that holds potent personal energy, signifying renewal and new beginnings. Perform it in the morning to set the tone for the day and the year ahead, or in the evening as a way to reflect on the past and set intentions for the future. If your birthday falls during a full moon or waxing moon, the spell's power will be further enhanced, as these phases support growth, illumination, and manifestation.

Steps for the Birthday Spell

1. Preparing the Sacred Space

Choose a quiet, comfortable area where you can perform the spell without interruption. Begin by cleansing the space with the bowl of sea salt water, sprinkling a few drops around you to purify the energy. Light the incense, allowing its smoke to swirl through the air, representing Libra's element and clearing away mental clutter.

Arrange the three candles in a triangle in front of you, with the pink candle at the top (representing Venus), the blue candle to the right (air and clarity), and the white candle to the left (purity and new beginnings). Place the bowl of rose petals and dried lavender near the candles, along with the mirror, parchment, pen, and pouch.

Take a moment to sit comfortably, close your eyes, and take several deep breaths, inhaling peace and exhaling tension. Visualize a soft pink light surrounding you, enveloping you in warmth and love as you prepare to set your intentions.

2. Reflecting on the Past Year

Hold the mirror in your hands and gaze into it. Take a few moments to reflect on the past year—your accomplishments, lessons learned, challenges faced, and the growth you have experienced. Acknowledge both the positive and the difficult aspects, as each has contributed to who you are today.

As you look into the mirror, say aloud or silently:

"I honor the year that has passed, the lessons learned, the love given, and the growth I have embraced. I am grateful for every experience that has brought me here."

Feel a sense of gratitude for your journey, recognizing the strengths and qualities you have developed over the past year.

3. Setting Your Intentions for the Year Ahead

Place the mirror down and pick up the piece of parchment or paper. Take a few moments to think about what you wish to manifest and cultivate in the coming year. Consider your goals, dreams, personal growth, and the type of energy you want to invite into your life. Write these intentions on the paper, being as specific or broad as feels right to you.

As you write, visualize each intention as a seed that you are planting in the fertile soil of the new year. See it growing, blossoming, and becoming a reality in your mind's eye. When you have finished, hold the paper to your heart and breathe deeply, infusing your intentions with love and determination.

4. Invoking Libra's Energy

Light the pink candle first, saying:

"By the light of Venus, I invoke love, beauty, and harmony into my life. May my intentions bloom with warmth and grace."

Next, light the blue candle, saying:

"By the power of air, I call upon clarity, inspiration, and communication. May my mind be clear and my words reflect truth."

Finally, light the white candle, saying:

"By the purity of this flame, I embrace new beginnings. May this year be filled with light, peace, and balance."

Feel the energy of the candles surrounding you, their light representing the paths you will walk in the year ahead.

5. Anointing the Intentions with Rose Petals and Lavender

Sprinkle a few rose petals and lavender over the parchment, saying:

"Rose petals, bring love and beauty to my desires. Lavender, bring peace, calm, and self-love to my journey."

Visualize the petals and lavender infusing the paper with their energies, nurturing your intentions and setting them on the path to manifestation.

6. Sealing the Intentions

Roll or fold the parchment containing your written intentions and place it inside the cloth pouch or envelope. Hold the pouch in your hands and close your eyes, focusing on the light of the candles. Picture the energy of the flames merging with the energy of your intentions, sealing them with the warmth and strength of your heart.

Whisper or say aloud:

"With love, I plant these seeds of intention. With light, I nurture them to grow. With balance, I walk the path ahead. This is my year; so mote it be."

Visualize the pouch glowing softly with a golden-pink light, representing the manifestation of your intentions throughout the year.

7. Concluding the Ritual

Place the pouch somewhere special, such as on your altar, in a drawer, or under your pillow, to keep your intentions close to you. Whenever you feel the need to reconnect with your goals and dreams, hold the pouch and reaffirm your intentions.

Blow out the candles one by one, saying:

"As this flame fades, my intentions take flight, guided by love, air, and light."

Allow the incense to continue burning if possible, letting its smoke carry your wishes into the universe.

8. Reflecting on the Ritual

After completing the spell, take a few moments to sit quietly and observe how you feel. Write down your experiences in your journal, including the intentions you set and any emotions or insights that surfaced during the ritual. Revisit these reflections throughout the year to track your progress and realign with your goals.

Tips for Enhancing the Birthday Spell

- **Renew the Pouch:** During the year, periodically revisit your intentions. If you feel your goals have changed or need adjustment, perform a mini-version of this ritual by writing down new intentions and placing them in the pouch.
- **Use Throughout the Year:** Keep the pouch in a place where you can access it easily. Whenever you need motivation, guidance, or a reminder of your intentions, hold the pouch and focus on its energy.
- **Celebrate Monthly:** Each month on the date of your birthday, light the candles again, and meditate on the progress of your intentions. This keeps the energy active and helps you stay aligned with your goals.

Final Thoughts

"The Birthday Spell: A Celebration of Self" is a powerful ritual that combines self-reflection, gratitude, and intention-setting to create a foundation for the year ahead. By drawing upon Libra's ruling elements—air and Venusian energy—you align your desires with the qualities of love, beauty, balance, and clarity, setting the stage for a year filled with growth and fulfillment.

This spell is not just about making wishes; it is a declaration of your commitment to personal development, self-love, and the pursuit of harmony. By celebrating your journey and defining your path forward, you take the reins of your destiny with grace and confidence. Each time you return to the pouch, you reaffirm your dedication to your goals, ensuring that the year ahead is guided by your intentions and the loving energy of Libra. With each birthday, you continue to evolve, building a life that reflects your inner beauty, balance, and aspirations.

Chapter 9: Moonlit Bath: Cleansing Ritual

Libras, ruled by the planet Venus, have a natural affinity for beauty, harmony, and balance. However, their constant striving for equilibrium can sometimes lead to mental exhaustion and emotional clutter. When the stresses of daily life and the energy of others accumulate, it can weigh heavily on a Libra's heart and mind, disrupting their sense of inner peace. The "Moonlit Bath: Cleansing Ritual" is designed to help you release these accumulated burdens and recharge your energy, using the purifying power of herbs, essential oils, and moonlight. This ritual draws on the moon's gentle and transformative energy to cleanse your body and soul, leaving you feeling refreshed, balanced, and reconnected to your inner harmony.

A cleansing bath ritual taps into the natural flow of water, the element that washes away impurities and restores a sense of calm. By infusing the bath with herbs and oils known for their purifying and calming properties, and performing the ritual under the moon's light, you amplify the bath's cleansing power, allowing it to wash away negativity and recharge your energy with the moon's serene illumination.

The Significance of Moonlight in the Cleansing Ritual

The moon, with its ever-changing phases, represents cycles of growth, release, and renewal. Its light carries a gentle yet powerful energy that can cleanse and recharge the spirit. Bathing in the moon's glow, whether directly under the night sky or with moon-charged water, connects you to these natural cycles, helping you release what no longer serves you and fill your being with tranquility and clarity.

Ingredients and Tools Needed

- Fresh or dried herbs: lavender (calming), rosemary (cleansing), chamomile (soothing), and rose petals (self-love)

- Essential oils: lavender, rose, or sandalwood (for calming and recharging)
- Sea salt or Epsom salt (for purification and grounding)
- A bowl or jar of moon-charged water (collected by placing a bowl of water under the moonlight overnight)
- A white or silver candle (to symbolize the moon and purity)
- A piece of moonstone or clear quartz (for enhancing the cleansing energy)
- Soft, soothing music (optional, for creating a relaxing atmosphere)
- A bathrobe or towel for after the bath
- A quiet, private bathroom
- A journal or notebook (to record reflections post-bath)

Timing the Ritual

Perform this ritual during a full moon or a waxing moon to harness the moon's cleansing and renewing power. The full moon is the most potent time for release and purification, while the waxing moon supports growth and recharging. For the best results, carry out this ritual in the evening when the moon is high, allowing you to bathe in its energy and illumination.

Steps for the Moonlit Bath Ritual

1. Preparing Your Bath Space

Begin by selecting a time when you will not be disturbed. Cleanse your bathroom beforehand, both physically and energetically. Wipe down the surfaces, tidy the space, and sprinkle sea salt around the bath area to purify it. Set up the white or silver candle near the bathtub, symbolizing the moon's light, and place the moonstone or clear quartz nearby to amplify the cleansing energy.

Turn off harsh lighting and, if possible, use only candles to light the room. If you have a window that allows moonlight to shine into the bathroom, open it to let the moon's energy fill the space. If not, trust that the moon's influence is still present in the ritual through the moon-charged water and your intention.

2. Preparing the Herbal Bath Mix

Gather the herbs—lavender, rosemary, chamomile, and rose petals—and place them in a small bowl. As you do so, focus on their individual properties:

- **Lavender:** Promotes relaxation, calmness, and peace of mind.
- **Rosemary:** Clears negativity, cleanses the aura, and sharpens mental clarity.
- **Chamomile:** Soothes emotional distress and invites inner tranquility.
- **Rose Petals:** Enhances self-love, compassion, and emotional harmony.

As you add each herb, say:

"By [herb's name], I call upon your power to cleanse, calm, and recharge my spirit."

Mix the herbs together with your hands, infusing them with your intention for a deep cleanse and renewal. Set the bowl aside.

3. Preparing the Moon-Charged Bath

Draw a warm bath, adding sea salt or Epsom salt to the water to further enhance its purifying properties. As the bath fills, add a few drops of the essential oil(s) of your choice—lavender for calmness, rose for self-love, or sandalwood for grounding. Then, add the herbal mix into the water, either directly or by placing it in a muslin bag if you prefer to avoid loose herbs in the tub.

Take the bowl of moon-charged water and pour it into the bath, saying:

"By the light of the moon, cleanse me through and through. Wash away all that hinders my peace, fill me with light, my energy's release."

Visualize the bathwater glowing softly, imbued with the moon's purifying and renewing energy.

4. Lighting the Candle and Setting the Intention

Light the white or silver candle, symbolizing the moon's glow, and place it where it can reflect on the water's surface. As you light the candle, say:

"Moon of purity, light of the night, cleanse my spirit, set it alight. Let this water wash away, all that's heavy, let peace now stay."

Close your eyes and take a few deep breaths, inhaling the calming scent of the herbs and oils, and exhaling any tension or negativity. Visualize the bath as a pool of moonlight, ready to cleanse and recharge you.

5. Entering the Bath and Soaking in the Moon's Energy

Slowly step into the bath, feeling the warmth of the water embrace you. As you sink into the water, allow yourself to relax completely, letting go of any stress or burdens you have been carrying. Close your eyes and imagine the water enveloping you in a cocoon of moonlight, gently washing away negativity, emotional clutter, and stagnant energy.

As you soak, reflect on anything you wish to release. You might think of emotions, thoughts, or experiences that no longer serve you. Visualize them dissolving into the water, transformed by the moon's energy into light.

Say the following affirmation:

"With each breath, I release; with each drop, I renew. The moonlight cleanses, the water heals. I am purified, balanced, and whole."

Spend as much time as you need in the bath, allowing yourself to fully embrace the sensation of being cleansed and recharged. If you wish, play soft, soothing music to enhance the atmosphere and deepen your relaxation.

6. Closing the Ritual and Sealing the Cleansing

When you feel ready to conclude the ritual, take the moonstone or clear quartz and hold it in your hand. Dip it into the bathwater briefly, then hold it to your heart, saying:

"Stone of light, keep me clear. The moon has cleansed, I hold it near. Balance and peace, now reside; with harmony and grace, I stride."

Carefully stand up and step out of the bath. Gently pat yourself dry with a towel or wrap yourself in a bathrobe. As you do so, imagine sealing the moon's energy into your skin, locking in the sense of clarity, peace, and balance.

7. Reflecting on the Experience

Once dressed, take a few moments to sit quietly. Notice how your body feels lighter, your mind clearer, and your spirit more at ease. Open your journal and write down your thoughts and feelings. Reflect on what you released during the bath and how the experience of cleansing has affected you.

Place the moonstone or clear quartz on your bedside table or altar to continue radiating its cleansing and recharging energy into your space.

8. Disposal of the Herbs

If you used loose herbs, collect them from the bathwater and return them to the earth, either by burying them in your garden or placing them at the base of a tree. This symbolizes the final release of any negativity you washed away and the return of that energy to nature for transformation.

Tips for Enhancing the Moonlit Bath Ritual

- **Charge Water in Moonlight:** If possible, collect water in a bowl and leave it outside or on a windowsill during the full or waxing moon to charge it with the moon's energy before the ritual.
- **Regular Practice:** Incorporate this ritual into your self-care routine monthly, especially during the full moon, to maintain emotional balance and energetic clarity.
- **Add Crystals:** If you feel drawn, you can add other crystals to the bath, such as amethyst for calming the mind or rose quartz for self-love.

Final Thoughts

The "Moonlit Bath: Cleansing Ritual" is a luxurious and deeply transformative way to cleanse your energy, release accumulated stress, and recharge your spirit. By using herbs, essential oils, and moonlight, you create a soothing environment that embodies Libra's love for beauty, harmony, and inner balance. This ritual is not just about physical cleansing; it is a holistic practice that purifies your emotional and mental states, leaving you feeling refreshed and in tune with your true self.

As a Libra, your quest for equilibrium often involves managing the energies of others and navigating life's complexities. This ritual offers a way to regularly reset your inner balance, aligning you with the moon's gentle yet powerful cycles. By immersing yourself in the moon's cleansing light, you honor your need for harmony, cultivate self-love, and prepare yourself to face the world with renewed clarity and grace.

Chapter 10: Venus' Embrace: Self-Love Spell

For Libras, ruled by Venus, self-love is a fundamental aspect of inner harmony and balance. Venus, the planet of love, beauty, and grace, endows Libra with the natural desire to create and maintain equilibrium in their surroundings and relationships. However, in their pursuit of harmony for others, Libras can sometimes overlook their own needs, leading to self-neglect and inner imbalance. "Venus' Embrace: Self-Love Spell" is designed to reconnect you with the loving energy of Venus, helping you to cultivate self-compassion, acceptance, and inner beauty. By working with rose quartz and Venus-themed incantations, this spell invokes the goddess's energy to fill your heart with unconditional love for yourself.

This spell focuses on invoking the gentle and nurturing energy of Venus to enhance self-worth, promote self-care, and embrace your unique qualities. It uses rose quartz, the stone of love and healing, to amplify the vibrations of self acceptance and compassion. Through this ritual, you will create a sacred space where you can nurture and honor your own essence, allowing Venus's embrace to remind you of your intrinsic worth and beauty.

The Power of Rose Quartz and Venusian Incantations

Rose quartz is known as the "Stone of Unconditional Love" and has long been associated with Venus. Its soothing pink hue embodies the essence of love, healing, and compassion. Rose quartz opens the heart chakra, allowing love to flow freely—both towards others and, importantly, towards oneself. In this spell, rose quartz serves as a focal point to help you channel Venus's energy, encouraging you to treat yourself with kindness and grace.

Venus-themed incantations further invoke the goddess's energy, allowing you to connect with her loving and transformative presence. These words of power are infused with Venusian qualities of beauty, harmony, and self-worth, enhancing your capacity for self-love.

Materials Needed

- A piece of rose quartz (for love, self-compassion, and healing)
- A pink candle (to symbolize Venus's loving energy)
- Rose petals (fresh or dried) or rose essential oil (to invoke the essence of Venus)
- A small bowl of honey (for sweetness and nurturing)
- A hand mirror (to reflect self-love and acceptance)
- A small piece of parchment or paper and a pink or red pen
- A cloth pouch (to create a self-love charm)
- A bowl of water mixed with sea salt (for purification)
- A quiet, comfortable space for the ritual
- A journal or notebook (to record reflections)

Timing the Spell

Perform this spell on a Friday, the day ruled by Venus, to maximize the influence of Venusian energy. The waxing or full moon is an ideal time for self-love rituals, as these lunar phases support growth, self-reflection, and the nurturing of positive emotions. Evening is a suitable time, allowing you to wind down, connect with your inner self, and embrace Venus's calming and loving energy.

Steps for the Self-Love Spell

1. Preparing the Sacred Space

Find a quiet, comfortable place where you can perform the ritual without interruptions. Begin by cleansing the space with the sea salt water, sprinkling it around the area to purify it and clear away any negative energy. Set up the pink candle in front of you, along with the rose quartz, rose petals (or rose essential oil), honey, mirror, parchment, and pen.

Light the pink candle, visualizing its flame as the light of Venus, shining down upon you and filling the space with warmth and love. Take a few deep breaths, inhaling calmness and self-compassion, and exhaling tension and self-criticism.

2. Connecting with Rose Quartz and Venus' Energy

Hold the rose quartz in your hands and close your eyes. Visualize a soft pink light emanating from the stone, enveloping you in a gentle embrace. Imagine this light coming from Venus herself, reaching out to you with unconditional love and acceptance. Feel the warmth of this energy flowing into your heart, dissolving any feelings of self-doubt or inadequacy.

With the rose quartz still in your hands, say:

"Venus, goddess of love and grace, I call upon your nurturing embrace. Fill my heart with love divine, for all of me, this love is mine."

Repeat this incantation until you feel the energy of Venus surrounding and supporting you. Allow this loving energy to settle into your heart, bringing with it a sense of peace and self-worth.

3. Writing Self-Love Affirmations

Take the piece of parchment or paper and the pink or red pen. Begin to write down affirmations that resonate with your desire for self-love and self-acceptance. These affirmations can include statements like:

- "I am worthy of love and kindness."
- "I embrace my unique qualities and honor my true self."
- "I am deserving of my own compassion and care."
- "I love and accept myself fully, just as I am."

Write each affirmation with intention and sincerity, feeling the truth of each word as you write. When you have finished, fold the parchment and hold it to your heart, allowing its words to resonate with the loving energy within you.

4. Anointing and Invoking Venus' Embrace

Place the folded parchment in front of the candle. Sprinkle a few rose petals over it, or anoint it with a drop of rose essential oil, saying:

"Rose of love, gentle and sweet, enhance my self-love, make it complete. With every petal, with every scent, I honor myself, my love's ascent."

Next, dip your finger into the bowl of honey and gently touch it to the parchment, symbolizing the sweetness you are inviting into your relationship with yourself. Say:

"Sweetness of honey, warmth of grace, I cherish myself in this sacred space. Venus, fill my heart with care, self-love blossoms, everywhere."

Visualize the parchment glowing softly, absorbing the energy of the rose petals, the honey, and the flame of the candle. Picture this light expanding, filling the entire space with a loving, nurturing energy that is directed toward you.

5. Gazing into the Mirror

Pick up the mirror and gaze into your own eyes. Look at yourself with compassion, as if seeing yourself through the loving eyes of Venus. Allow any judgments or negative thoughts to dissipate, replaced by an understanding and acceptance of who you are.

As you continue to gaze into the mirror, say:

"In this reflection, I see the truth, beauty within, both old and youth. Venus, grant me eyes to see, the love I give is also for me."

Hold this gaze for a few moments, allowing the words to sink in. Feel the energy of Venus flowing through the mirror, filling you with a profound sense of self-love and worth.

6. Creating the Self-Love Charm

Take the parchment, rose quartz, and a few rose petals, and place them inside the cloth pouch. Hold the pouch in your hands, close to your heart, and say:

"By Venus' light, by rose and stone, I embrace the love that is my own. This charm I keep, close to me, a reminder of my worth, blessed by thee."

Visualize the pouch glowing with a soft pink light, infused with the energy of the spell. This charm will serve as a reminder of your self-worth and the love you have cultivated for yourself during this ritual.

7. Sealing the Spell

Gently blow out the candle, allowing its smoke to carry your intention for self-love to the universe. As you extinguish the flame, say:

"As this light fades, my love shines bright. In Venus' embrace, I hold this light. So mote it be."

Keep the charm pouch somewhere special, such as under your pillow, in your bag, or on your bedside table. Whenever you need a reminder of your worth and self-love, hold the pouch and reconnect with the energy of the spell.

8. Reflecting on the Ritual

After completing the spell, sit quietly and take a few moments to reflect on how you feel. Notice any sensations of warmth, peace, or newfound appreciation for yourself. Write down your experience in your journal, including the affirmations you set and any emotions or insights that surfaced during the ritual.

Tips for Enhancing the Self-Love Spell

- **Use Regularly:** This spell can be performed whenever you need a boost of self-love and self-acceptance. Repeating the ritual strengthens the energy of self-compassion within you.
- **Carry the Rose Quartz:** Keep the rose quartz with you as a reminder of your self-love, and hold it during times of self-doubt or emotional turbulence to reconnect with Venus's energy.
- **Daily Affirmations:** Each morning, hold the charm pouch and recite one of your written affirmations to reinforce the spell's influence and start your day with a sense of self-worth.

Final Thoughts

"Venus' Embrace: Self-Love Spell" is a nurturing ritual that reconnects you with the loving energy of Venus, reminding you of your inherent worth and beauty. By using rose quartz and Venus-themed incantations, you open your heart to the goddess's grace, allowing her to fill you with the warmth and acceptance that fosters self-love.

As a Libra, your pursuit of harmony often begins with how you treat yourself. This spell serves as a reminder that self-love is not selfish but essential for maintaining balance and peace in your life. By embracing Venus's light within, you become more attuned to your needs, more compassionate toward yourself, and more capable of sharing your love with the world. Carry the energy of this spell with you, and let it guide you on your journey toward deeper self-care, appreciation, and inner harmony.

Chapter 11: Feather of Ma'at: Decision-Making Spell

Libras are known for their strong desire for balance, fairness, and harmony. While these qualities make them adept at seeing multiple perspectives, they can also make decision-making a challenge. Torn between options and considerations, Libras often struggle to choose a path, fearing that one choice might disrupt the balance they so carefully maintain. The "Feather of Ma'at: Decision-Making Spell" is designed to aid in these moments of indecision. By invoking the ancient Egyptian goddess Ma'at, who embodies truth, balance, and justice, this spell taps into your inner wisdom to help you weigh your choices with clarity and confidence.

This ritual uses a feather, a symbol of Ma'at and the lightness of truth, as well as the flame of a candle to illuminate the path of your decision-making process. By channeling Ma'at's energy, you align with the universal principles of truth and justice, allowing you to connect with your higher self and access the wisdom needed to make the best decision. This spell is not about forcing a choice; it is about bringing to light the option that resonates most deeply with your values and inner truth.

The Symbolism of the Feather and Candle Flame

In ancient Egyptian mythology, the goddess Ma'at presides over truth, balance, and cosmic order. Her symbol, the feather, represents the lightness of truth and the ideal of weighing the heart against the feather to assess one's purity. Similarly, the candle flame represents illumination, clarity, and the guidance of one's inner light. By incorporating these elements into the spell, you invoke the energy of Ma'at to bring clarity, honesty, and balance to your decision-making process.

Materials Needed

- A feather (preferably a white or natural-colored feather to symbolize Ma'at's purity and truth)
- A white candle (to represent clarity, truth, and the light of inner wisdom)
- A piece of parchment or paper and a pen

- A small bowl of water mixed with sea salt (for purification)
- A small dish or tray (to place the feather on during the spell)
- A quiet, undisturbed space for the ritual
- A journal or notebook (to record reflections and outcomes)

Timing the Spell

This spell can be performed at any time when you are facing a difficult decision. However, it is most effective during a waxing moon, as this phase supports growth, insight, and the development of new directions. For added harmony, perform this spell on a Wednesday, ruled by Mercury, the planet of communication and intellect, to enhance mental clarity and decision-making skills.

Steps for the Decision-Making Spell

1. Preparing the Sacred Space

Choose a quiet, comfortable area where you will not be disturbed. Begin by cleansing the space with the sea salt water, sprinkling a few drops around you to purify the environment and clear any lingering energies that may cloud your judgment. Set up the candle in front of you, along with the feather, parchment, pen, and a small dish or tray to hold the feather during the ritual.

Light the candle, focusing on its flame. Visualize it as a beacon of clarity and truth, illuminating the darkness of indecision. Allow the candle's light to fill the room, creating a circle of calm and focus around you.

2. Setting Your Intentions

Sit comfortably and take several deep breaths, inhaling calmness and exhaling any anxiety or confusion related to your decision. Hold the feather in your hands, feeling its lightness and softness. Visualize it glowing with a soft white light, representing the energy of Ma'at and the purity of truth.

Close your eyes and focus on the decision you need to make. Picture the different options you are considering, and allow any emotions, thoughts, or concerns related to each option to surface. As you hold the feather, say the following affirmation:

"Ma'at, goddess of truth and balance, I call upon your guidance. Grant me the clarity to see the truth, the balance to weigh my choices, and the wisdom to choose what aligns with my highest good."

Repeat this affirmation until you feel a sense of calm and connection with Ma'at's energy.

3. Writing Down the Options

Take the parchment or paper and pen. Write down the options you are considering, listing them clearly. If there are pros and cons associated with each choice, feel free to note them briefly. This exercise helps to externalize your thoughts, providing a clearer perspective on the options before you.

When you have finished writing, fold the paper and place it on the dish or tray. Then, gently place the feather on top of the folded paper, symbolizing Ma'at's feather of truth weighing upon the choices you have laid out.

4. The Candle and Feather Ritual

Focus on the feather resting on the paper. Envision it as Ma'at's feather, light yet full of profound wisdom. The feather represents the truth you seek in making your decision. It will help weigh the options without the burden of fear, doubt, or bias.

Gaze into the flame of the candle and allow your mind to quiet. Imagine the flame burning away confusion and illuminating the path that best aligns with your truth and inner wisdom. Visualize the candlelight expanding, surrounding the feather and paper with a gentle glow.

Say the following incantation:

"Feather of Ma'at, light and true, guide my heart, show what to do. By flame's light and Ma'at's grace, reveal the path I'm meant to embrace."

Keep your gaze on the candle flame, allowing your mind to remain open and receptive. Notice any thoughts, feelings, or impressions that come to you. You may experience a sense of knowing, a pull toward one option, or an insight that shifts your perspective.

5. Holding the Feather for Inner Wisdom

After a few minutes of contemplation, gently pick up the feather and hold it to your heart. Close your eyes and take a deep breath, focusing on the feather's lightness. This act symbolizes weighing your heart against the feather of Ma'at, seeking the decision that feels light, true, and in harmony with your inner values.

As you hold the feather, silently ask yourself:

"Which choice aligns with my truth? What decision brings balance to my life and spirit?"

Pay attention to your feelings, instincts, and bodily sensations. Trust the insights that arise, whether they come as a feeling of ease toward a particular choice or a sense of certainty. The feather serves as a conduit for your inner wisdom, helping you discern the path that resonates with your higher self.

6. Sealing the Decision

When you feel ready, place the feather back on the dish. Acknowledge the clarity and guidance you have received, even if you do not yet have a clear answer. Sometimes, the spell serves to open the door for further reflection and insight in the days to come.

Say the closing affirmation:

"By Ma'at's feather, light and just, I honor the truth, I honor my trust. The path I choose shall be aligned, with clarity, peace, and heart combined. So mote it be."

Gently blow out the candle, allowing the smoke to carry your intention for balance and clarity to the universe. Keep the feather in a safe place, such as on an altar or within a book, to serve as a reminder of Ma'at's guidance whenever you face future decisions.

7. Reflecting on the Ritual

After completing the spell, take a few moments to sit quietly and reflect on how you feel. Write down any insights, feelings, or impressions you received during the ritual in your journal. If you have not yet made a decision, trust that further clarity will come to you in the following days. This ritual may open your mind to signs, synchronicities, and intuitive nudges that guide you toward the best path.

Tips for Enhancing Decision-Making Clarity

- **Use the Feather Regularly:** Whenever you feel indecisive or overwhelmed, hold the feather in your hands, close your eyes, and recite a shortened version of the incantation to reconnect with Ma'at's wisdom.
- **Meditate with the Feather:** Use the feather as a focal point during meditation to enhance mental clarity and align with your inner truth.
- **Sleep on It:** If you remain unsure after the ritual, place the feather under your pillow and ask for Ma'at's guidance in your dreams. Insights may come to you while you sleep.

Final Thoughts

The "Feather of Ma'at: Decision-Making Spell" is a powerful way to tap into your inner wisdom and bring balance to the decision making process. By invoking the energy of Ma'at and using the symbols of the feather and candle flame, you create a sacred space where your mind can clear, your heart can speak, and the truth can emerge. This spell aligns with Libra's quest for fairness and harmony, offering a method to weigh options thoughtfully and choose the path that resonates with your higher self.

Decision-making is not always about finding the perfect answer, but rather about making a choice that aligns with your values, intuition, and truth. With Ma'at's feather as your guide, you empower yourself to navigate life's complexities with a heart that is light, a mind that is clear, and a spirit that is in harmony.

Chapter 12: Aura Harmonization: Protection Spell

For Libras, maintaining harmony and balance in their personal energy is crucial. As social beings, Libras are naturally attuned to the energies of those around them. However, this sensitivity can make them more susceptible to negative influences and energetic disruptions, leading to emotional fatigue, stress, and imbalance. "Aura Harmonization: Protection Spell" is designed to cleanse and shield your aura, helping you maintain your personal equilibrium amidst the chaos of daily life. This spell employs specific crystals and herbs known for their protective and harmonizing properties, creating a powerful shield that purifies and safeguards your energy.

An aura, often seen as a glowing field of energy surrounding a person, reflects one's physical, emotional, and spiritual state. A clean and balanced aura promotes clarity, well-being, and a sense of peace, while an aura clouded with negativity can lead to feelings of confusion, anxiety, and emotional unrest. This spell works to clear away any accumulated negative energies and fortify your aura with a protective shield, allowing you to navigate interactions and environments with confidence and inner stability.

Crystals and Herbs for Aura Protection and Cleansing

Crystals and herbs have long been used in spellcraft for their unique vibrational properties and their abilities to cleanse, protect, and harmonize energy fields. In this spell, you will use a combination of crystals and herbs selected for their protective qualities:

- **Black Tourmaline:** A grounding crystal that absorbs and repels negative energy. It serves as a protective barrier, helping to keep your aura clear and balanced.
- **Amethyst:** Known for its calming and purifying properties, amethyst enhances spiritual awareness and creates a protective field around your energy.

- **Rosemary:** An herb associated with purification, mental clarity, and protective magic. It cleanses the aura and repels unwanted influences.
- **Sage:** One of the most potent herbs for purification, sage is used to clear negativity and promote an environment of peace and balance.
- **Lavender:** Promotes calmness and serenity, soothing the aura and providing an additional layer of gentle protection.

By combining these elements, you create a spell that not only cleanses your aura but also strengthens it against negative influences.

Materials Needed

- A black tourmaline crystal (for protection and grounding)
- An amethyst crystal (for calming and spiritual protection)
- Dried rosemary (for cleansing and mental clarity)
- Dried sage (for purification)
- Dried lavender (for calmness and aura harmonization)
- A white candle (to symbolize purity and light)
- A small bowl of water mixed with sea salt (for purification)
- A small pouch or cloth bag (to create a protective charm)
- A fireproof bowl or cauldron (for burning herbs)
- A feather or fan (to waft the herb smoke around your aura)
- A quiet, comfortable space for the ritual
- A journal or notebook (to record reflections)

Timing the Spell

The best time to perform this spell is during a waning moon, as this phase supports the release of negative energies and the creation of protective boundaries. For added potency, perform the ritual on a Saturday, a day ruled by Saturn, which governs protection, boundaries, and grounding. Evening is an ideal time, as the setting sun symbolizes the closing of a day and the establishment of a protective barrier for the night and the days to come.

Steps for the Aura Harmonization Spell

1. Preparing the Sacred Space

Begin by selecting a quiet, undisturbed area where you can perform the spell. Cleanse the space using the bowl of water mixed with sea salt, sprinkling a few drops around the area to purify the energy. Set up the white candle in front of you to represent purity and light, and arrange the crystals, herbs, feather, pouch, and fireproof bowl nearby.

Light the white candle and take a moment to focus on its flame. Visualize the light filling the room, creating a circle of protection and peace around you. This sacred space will serve as the center of the cleansing and protective energies you are about to invoke.

2. Setting Your Intentions

Sit comfortably and hold the black tourmaline and amethyst crystals in your hands. Close your eyes and take several deep breaths, inhaling calmness and exhaling any stress or tension. Focus on your aura, envisioning it as a glowing field of light surrounding your body. Notice if there are any areas that feel heavy, dark, or disrupted.

Set your intention for the spell, silently or aloud, saying:

"I call upon the energies of protection and harmony. Cleanse my aura of all negativity, and fortify my shield against all harm. Let peace, balance, and light fill my being."

Repeat this affirmation until you feel centered and connected to your intention.

3. Creating the Herbal Smoke Blend

In the fireproof bowl or cauldron, combine the dried rosemary, sage, and lavender. As you add each herb, focus on its properties:

- **Rosemary:** Sprinkle it into the bowl while saying, *"Rosemary, cleanse and clear, repel all shadows that come near."*
- **Sage:** Add to the bowl while saying, *"Sage, pure and true, purify my aura, renew."*

- **Lavender:** Add to the bowl while saying, *"Lavender, calm and bright, surround my aura with peaceful light."*

As you mix the herbs, visualize them glowing with a protective light, ready to cleanse and harmonize your aura.

4. Cleansing and Shielding the Aura

Light the herbal blend in the fireproof bowl, allowing it to smolder and produce smoke. Pick up the feather or fan and use it to waft the smoke around your body, starting at your feet and moving upward to the crown of your head. As you do this, envision the smoke penetrating your aura, dissolving any negativity and filling you with a sense of peace and protection.

As you waft the smoke, say the following incantation:

"Smoke of sage, rosemary, and bloom, cleanse my aura, clear the gloom. Lavender's calm, tourmaline's might, surround me now with protective light."

Continue moving the smoke around your body, paying extra attention to any areas where you sensed heaviness or disruption. Visualize these areas being purified and harmonized, replaced with a glowing, radiant energy.

5. Charging the Crystals for Protection

After completing the smoke cleansing, place the black tourmaline and amethyst crystals in front of the candle. Focus on the candle's flame and imagine it infusing the crystals with protective energy.

Pick up the black tourmaline and hold it to your heart, saying:

"Black tourmaline, shield and ground, keep my aura safe and sound."

Next, pick up the amethyst and hold it to your third eye, saying:

"Amethyst, calm and pure, surround me with a shield secure."

Visualize both crystals glowing brightly, charged with the intention to protect and balance your aura.

6. Creating the Protection Charm

Place the charged crystals into the cloth pouch, along with a pinch of the remaining herbal blend. Hold the pouch in your hands and close your eyes. Visualize a bright, protective light emanating from the pouch, expanding outward to form a shield around your entire aura.

Say the following affirmation to seal the charm:

"This charm I hold, with herbs and stone, guards my aura, my sacred throne. By earth and light, my shield is strong, I walk in peace, where I belong."

Keep this pouch with you, in your bag or pocket, to serve as a protective amulet that continuously fortifies your aura.

7. Sealing the Spell

Gently blow out the candle, allowing the smoke to carry your intention for protection and harmony to the universe. As you extinguish the flame, say:

"By the light of this flame, I seal my shield. My aura is cleansed, my protection revealed. So mote it be."

Place the pouch in a safe place or carry it with you to maintain the spell's protective influence.

8. Reflecting on the Ritual

Sit quietly for a few moments and observe how you feel. Notice any sensations of lightness, clarity, or a renewed sense of peace. Write down your experience in your journal, reflecting on how the ritual has affected your state of mind and energy.

Tips for Enhancing Aura Protection

- **Recharge the Pouch:** Place the pouch under a full moon or near a white candle to recharge its protective energy periodically.
- **Daily Aura Maintenance:** Each morning, hold the pouch and visualize your aura as a glowing, protective shield. This daily practice reinforces the spell's influence and maintains the aura's harmony.
- **Cleansing Baths:** Incorporate sea salt, rosemary, and lavender into your regular baths to cleanse your aura and recharge your energy.

Final Thoughts

The "Aura Harmonization: Protection Spell" is a powerful ritual designed to cleanse and fortify your aura against negative influences. By using specific crystals and herbs, you align with the energies of purification, calmness, and protection, creating a harmonious shield around your energy field. This spell resonates deeply with Libra's natural inclination toward balance and peace, providing a means to maintain personal equilibrium amidst life's uncertainties.

As you carry this spell's protective energy with you, you strengthen your inner harmony and resilience. Remember, a balanced aura is not just about warding off negativity but also about creating a space where your true self can thrive. With this spell, you honor your need for harmony, embrace your protective strength, and walk through the world with the confidence and peace of a well-shielded aura.

Chapter 13: Libran Garden: Herb-Growing Spell

Libras have a natural connection to beauty, harmony, and the nurturing of relationships, which extends into their love for gardening. Growing herbs, especially those associated with Libra, is a wonderful way to cultivate inner balance and harmony while connecting with the earth's rhythms. "Libran Garden: Herb-Growing Spell" is designed to enhance the growth of herbs that resonate with Libra's energy, such as rosemary, thyme, mint, lavender, and catnip. By performing this spell, you create a sacred space that not only nurtures these plants but also strengthens your own sense of peace, balance, and well-being.

Herb gardening has long been considered a form of natural magic, where each herb carries its own unique energy and properties. In this spell, you will plant and nurture a garden infused with your intentions for growth, harmony, and beauty. By combining the physical act of gardening with the magical influence of Libra's ruling planet, Venus, you align the garden with your zodiac's energy, allowing the herbs to flourish while enriching your own life with their vibrant presence.

Understanding Libra's Herbal Allies

Several herbs are associated with Libra due to their Venusian qualities of love, beauty, harmony, and balance. Here are a few key herbs to include in your Libran garden:

- **Rosemary:** Associated with mental clarity, purification, and protection, rosemary enhances peace and calm in a Libran's life.
- **Thyme:** Known for its connection to courage, strength, and purification, thyme supports a Libra's pursuit of balance and mental focus.
- **Mint:** Fresh and invigorating, mint promotes mental clarity and soothing energy, qualities that resonate with Libra's desire for balance and serenity.

- **Lavender:** A symbol of calmness, beauty, and tranquility, lavender helps soothe Libra's sometimes overactive mind, promoting inner harmony.
- **Catnip:** Connected to relaxation, love, and friendship, catnip aligns with Libra's social and affectionate nature.

Materials Needed

- Seeds or small plants of Libra-associated herbs (rosemary, thyme, mint, lavender, and catnip)
- Small pots or a garden bed for planting
- A small trowel or gardening spade
- Organic soil mix (preferably enriched with compost)
- A watering can filled with moon-charged water (collected by placing a bowl of water under the moonlight overnight)
- Crystals: rose quartz (for love and harmony), clear quartz (for energy amplification)
- A white or green candle (to represent growth, harmony, and Venusian energy)
- A bowl of dried lavender (to sprinkle around the plants)
- A piece of parchment or paper and a pen (to write your intentions)
- A quiet outdoor space for planting
- A journal or notebook (to record your gardening experience)

Timing the Spell

This spell is best performed during a waxing moon phase, as the moon's growing light supports the sprouting and growth of new life. For added influence, perform the ritual on a Friday, the day ruled by Venus, to enhance the harmony and love infused into your garden. Ideally, carry out the spell during the morning or early afternoon when the sun is rising, as this symbolizes the beginning of growth and life.

Steps for the Herb-Growing Spell
1. Preparing the Planting Space

Choose a spot in your garden or select pots that will receive ample sunlight, as most Libra-associated herbs thrive in sunny conditions. Cleanse the space by sprinkling a little bit of sea salt or dried lavender around the area to purify it, setting the intention that this is a sacred place for growth and harmony.

Gather your materials: seeds or plants, pots or garden bed, trowel, soil, watering can with moon-charged water, crystals, candle, parchment, and pen. Light the candle and place it nearby to represent the nurturing energy of Venus that will watch over the garden.

2. Setting Your Intentions for the Garden

Before planting, take a moment to connect with the earth beneath your feet. Close your eyes, take a deep breath, and feel the energy of the soil, the sunlight, and the air around you. Visualize the garden filled with lush, healthy herbs growing harmoniously, each radiating the beauty and balance you wish to bring into your life.

Take the piece of parchment and write down your intentions for this garden. For example, you might write: "May these herbs grow strong and vibrant, bringing harmony, peace, and balance into my life." Include specific wishes for each herb, such as clarity for rosemary, courage for thyme, and relaxation for lavender.

When you have finished writing, fold the parchment and place it in the soil at the center of the planting area or at the base of one of the pots. This will serve as a grounding point for your intentions as the herbs grow.

3. Planting the Herbs

Using the trowel, dig small holes for each herb. As you plant the seeds or small plants, hold each one in your hands for a moment and focus on its unique qualities:

- **Rosemary:** As you plant rosemary, say: *"Rosemary, herb of clarity and peace, grow strong and true, bring calm release."*
- **Thyme:** As you plant thyme, say: *"Thyme, bring courage, strength, and light, fill this garden with your might."*
- **Mint:** As you plant mint, say: *"Mint, fresh and soothing, cleanse the air, bring clarity and balance, beyond compare."*
- **Lavender:** As you plant lavender, say: *"Lavender, calm and serene, weave harmony through leaves of green."*
- **Catnip:** As you plant catnip, say: *"Catnip, love, and joy you bring, grow in peace, let your energy sing."*

Place the seeds or plants into the soil and cover them gently with earth, patting it down to secure each one in place. As you plant, visualize each herb glowing with a soft light, representing the life force within them that is now being nurtured.

4. Adding Crystals for Growth and Harmony

Place the rose quartz and clear quartz crystals around the garden bed or at the edges of the pots. Rose quartz, with its loving vibrations, will infuse the garden with Venusian energy, while clear quartz will amplify the growth and harmony of the herbs.

As you position each crystal, say:

"Crystals of love and light, nurture this garden, keep it bright. By Venus' grace and earth's embrace, let harmony and growth take place."

5. Watering with Moon-Charged Water

Take the watering can filled with moon-charged water and begin to water the newly planted herbs. As the water flows, visualize it glowing with the light of the moon, nourishing the seeds and plants with its energy.

As you water, recite the following incantation:

"Water of the moon, feed this ground, bring life and love, let growth abound. With each drop, harmony flows, as these herbs take root and grow."

Feel the connection between the water, the earth, and the growing plants, knowing that each element works together to bring life and balance to the garden.

6. Sprinkling Lavender for Protection

Once you have finished watering, take the dried lavender and sprinkle it around the base of the plants or at the edges of the pots. This will act as a natural protective barrier, warding off negativity and pests while enhancing the garden's peaceful atmosphere.

As you sprinkle the lavender, say:

"Lavender of peace, guard this place, keep it safe in Venus' grace. Let these herbs grow strong and free, in balance, love, and harmony."

7. Concluding the Ritual

Stand quietly by the garden and take a moment to sense the energy you have created. Imagine the herbs growing vibrantly, their leaves reaching toward the sky, embodying the balance and harmony of Libra. Thank the earth, the water, the crystals, and the moon for their assistance in nurturing your garden.

Blow out the candle, saying:

"With this flame's end, my spell is sealed. Growth and balance now revealed. By Venus' light and nature's might, this garden grows, pure and bright. So mote it be."

8. Reflecting on the Experience

After completing the ritual, write down your experience in your journal. Note how you felt during the planting process, the intentions you set, and any impressions you received. Throughout the growing season, revisit your journal to track the garden's progress and your own personal growth.

Tips for Enhancing the Herb-Growing Spell

- **Tend Your Garden Regularly:** Spend time each day caring for your garden. As you water, prune, and harvest the herbs, repeat affirmations of growth and harmony to reinforce the spell's energy.

- **Harvest with Intention:** When harvesting herbs, do so with gratitude and intention. Thank the plant for its gifts and ask that it continue to grow and provide.
- **Use the Herbs in Spells and Rituals:** Incorporate your home-grown herbs into spells, teas, or baths to connect with their energies and amplify their magical properties.

Final Thoughts

The "Libran Garden: Herb-Growing Spell" is a beautiful and transformative ritual that merges the practical aspects of gardening with the magical energies of Libra. By planting and nurturing a garden of herbs associated with your zodiac sign, you create a living symbol of balance, harmony, and growth. As the herbs flourish, so too will your connection to Venusian energy and your own inner equilibrium.

Gardening is more than just a physical act; it is a form of self-care and spiritual practice that allows you to cultivate not only plants but also the qualities you wish to embody. Through this spell, you align with the natural cycles of the earth and the moon, deepening your relationship with nature and the harmonious spirit of Libra. As your garden grows, let it remind you of your own potential for growth, beauty, and balance in all areas of life.

Chapter 14: Venus Mirror: Glamour and Charm Spell

For a Libra, charm, beauty, and confidence are deeply tied to Venus, the planet of love, beauty, and attraction. Libra's natural grace and social acumen are gifts bestowed by this ruling planet. However, there are times when even the most self-assured Libra might need a boost in their charm and confidence. The "Venus Mirror: Glamour and Charm Spell" is designed to invoke the energy of Venus, using mirrors as a conduit to reflect and amplify your inner beauty and magnetism. This spell harnesses Venusian energy to enhance your charm, promote self-love, and project an aura of confidence that draws others to you.

In the world of magic, mirrors are powerful tools for reflection, amplification, and self-perception. They not only show us our physical appearance but also serve as portals to our inner selves. By combining mirrors with Venusian energy, you create a spell that infuses your reflection with love, beauty, and self-assurance, enabling you to step into the world with greater confidence and charisma.

The Power of Venusian Energy and Mirrors

Venus governs love, beauty, harmony, and attraction, making its energy essential for glamour spells that enhance charm and confidence. Mirrors, on the other hand, represent self-reflection and projection, allowing you to work with your self-image and influence how others perceive you. In this spell, you will use a mirror to channel Venusian energy into your reflection, creating an aura of irresistible charm that resonates with your inner beauty.

Materials Needed

- A hand mirror or small vanity mirror (clean and free of smudges)
- A pink candle (to symbolize Venus's loving energy)
- Rose petals or rose essential oil (to invoke Venusian qualities)
- A piece of rose quartz (for love, self-confidence, and beauty)
- A bowl of water (preferably moon-charged by placing it under moonlight overnight)

- A piece of parchment or paper and a pink pen (to write affirmations)
- A soft cloth (to cleanse the mirror)
- A quiet, comfortable space for the ritual
- A journal or notebook (to record reflections)

Timing the Spell

This spell is most effective when performed on a Friday, the day ruled by Venus, which enhances love, beauty, and charm. For added potency, perform the ritual during a waxing or full moon to magnify your intentions for confidence and attraction. Evening is a suitable time, as dusk signifies the transition from day to night, reflecting the spell's aim to shift and amplify your inner glow.

Steps for the Glamour and Charm Spell

1. Preparing the Sacred Space

Find a quiet, comfortable space where you can perform the spell without interruption. Begin by cleansing the area with the moon-charged water, sprinkling a few drops around the space to purify it and create a circle of harmonious energy. Place the pink candle, rose petals (or rose essential oil), rose quartz, mirror, and parchment within reach.

Light the pink candle, visualizing its flame as the loving, radiant light of Venus. Allow the candle's warmth to fill the space, creating an atmosphere of beauty, love, and self-acceptance.

2. Cleansing the Mirror

Take the soft cloth and dip it into the moon-charged water. Gently wipe the surface of the mirror, saying:

"Mirror of Venus, clear and bright, cleanse away shadows, reflect the light. Let this surface pure and true, show my charm in every view."

As you cleanse the mirror, visualize it absorbing the moon's energy, becoming a vessel for the Venusian magic you are about to invoke.

3. Setting Your Intentions for Glamour and Confidence

Close your eyes and hold the rose quartz in your hands. Focus on its soft, loving energy and visualize a warm pink light emanating from it, enveloping your entire being. This light is the essence of Venus, enhancing your natural beauty and filling you with self-assurance.

Hold this vision in your mind and think about the qualities of charm, confidence, and beauty you wish to project. Set your intention for the spell by saying:

"Venus, goddess of love and grace, I call upon your light to fill this space. Grant me charm, beauty, and confidence true, let my inner glow shine through."

Repeat this affirmation until you feel your intention solidify, resonating with the energy around you.

4. Writing Affirmations of Charm and Confidence

Take the piece of parchment and the pink pen. Write down affirmations that embody the qualities you wish to enhance in yourself. These affirmations might include:

- "I radiate beauty and charm effortlessly."
- "I am confident in my unique beauty and presence."
- "My inner light shines brightly, attracting love and admiration."
- "I embrace my charm and project it with confidence."

Write each affirmation with intention, allowing the energy of Venus to infuse every word. Once you have finished, fold the parchment and place it near the candle.

5. Invoking Venus' Energy Through the Mirror

Hold the mirror in your hands and gaze into it. Look into your own eyes and focus on the beauty and uniqueness of your reflection. Allow any negative thoughts or self-doubts to surface, and then gently release them, acknowledging that they do not define your worth or beauty.

Place the rose quartz on the back of the mirror and hold them both together, saying:

"Mirror of Venus, reflect my grace, reveal my charm in every space. Rose quartz of love, enhance my glow, let my confidence and beauty show."

Visualize the mirror glowing with a soft pink light, filling with the loving and harmonious energy of Venus. Picture this light seeping into your reflection, transforming it into one of radiant charm and self-assurance.

6. Performing the Glamour Ritual

Hold the mirror up to your face and, as you gaze at your reflection, recite each affirmation you wrote aloud, one by one. Speak the words with conviction, as though you are declaring them to the universe. With each affirmation, visualize your reflection becoming more vibrant, your eyes shining with confidence, and your aura glowing with an irresistible charm.

After reciting the affirmations, place the mirror down and sprinkle a few rose petals around it. If using rose essential oil, anoint the mirror's edges with a small amount, saying:

"By Venus' light and rose's bloom, I enchant my reflection, dispel the gloom. Beauty within, beauty I show, charm and confidence now overflow."

Close your eyes and visualize your entire being surrounded by the pink light of Venus. Feel this energy radiating outward, creating an aura of beauty and charm that others cannot help but notice.

7. Sealing the Spell

To seal the spell, gently blow out the candle, allowing the smoke to carry your intention for glamour and confidence to the universe. As you extinguish the flame, say:

"By Venus' light, my charm is sealed. My beauty shines, my confidence revealed. As I will, so mote it be."

Keep the mirror in a special place, such as on your vanity or altar. Whenever you need a boost of charm or confidence, use the mirror to reconnect with the spell's energy.

8. Reflecting on the Ritual

After completing the spell, take a few moments to sit quietly and reflect on how you feel. Notice any sensations of warmth, self-love, or enhanced confidence. Write down your experience in your journal, including the affirmations you used and any insights or emotions that surfaced during the ritual.

Tips for Enhancing the Glamour and Charm Spell

- **Daily Mirror Affirmations:** Use the mirror each morning to repeat your affirmations, reinforcing the spell's energy and setting a positive tone for the day.
- **Carry the Rose Quartz:** Keep the rose quartz with you as a reminder of Venus's loving energy and the charm and confidence you have invoked.
- **Refresh the Spell Monthly:** Perform this spell regularly, especially during the waxing moon, to maintain and amplify your aura of glamour and charm.

Final Thoughts

The "Venus Mirror: Glamour and Charm Spell" is a powerful way to invoke the energy of Venus to enhance your natural beauty, charm, and confidence. By using the mirror as a tool for self-reflection and projection, you align with the loving and magnetic qualities of your ruling planet, creating an aura that radiates outward and draws others to you.

For Libras, who are naturally attuned to the desire for harmony and beauty, this spell serves as a reminder that true charm comes from embracing one's unique qualities and projecting them with confidence. It is not about changing who you are, but about amplifying the grace and light that already reside within you. As you gaze into the mirror, let Venus's energy remind you of your worth, your beauty, and the endless charm that you carry with you every day.

Chapter 15: Sweet Balance: Emotional Healing Spell

Libras, ruled by Venus, are naturally inclined towards harmony, beauty, and balance. However, their quest for equilibrium can often lead them to internalize emotions, seeking to keep the peace even when they are hurting. Emotional wounds can disrupt their inner harmony, creating a sense of imbalance that is hard to shake off. The "Sweet Balance: Emotional Healing Spell" is designed to address this need for emotional healing and comfort, using the nurturing qualities of sweet foods and honey to restore inner peace and self-love. This spell embraces the gentle, comforting energy of Venus to soothe emotional pain and promote a sense of sweetness and warmth within the soul.

In magic, sweet foods and honey are powerful symbols of love, comfort, and joy. They not only provide physical nourishment but also serve as reminders of life's simple pleasures. By incorporating these elements into the spell, you tap into their healing properties, using sweetness to mend emotional wounds, dispel negativity, and restore a sense of balance and harmony. This spell creates a space where you can nurture yourself, allowing the soothing energy of Venus to envelop you in warmth and compassion.

The Magic of Sweet Foods and Honey

Sweet foods and honey have long been associated with love magic, healing, and emotional comfort. Honey, often called "nectar of the gods," is linked to Venus for its sweetness, nurturing properties, and golden hue that symbolizes the light of love. When used in spellwork, honey acts as a balm for the soul, sealing wounds and promoting emotional balance. Pairing honey with sweet foods, like fruits, pastries, or chocolate, amplifies the spell's energy, creating a sensory experience that invokes feelings of joy, warmth, and self-care.

Materials Needed

- A small bowl of honey (for sweetness, healing, and self-love)
- Sweet foods of your choice (such as fresh fruit, pastries, chocolate, or a small piece of cake)
- A pink candle (to represent love, comfort, and Venus's nurturing energy)
- Rose petals or rose essential oil (to invoke the soothing energy of Venus)
- A small dish of sugar (to enhance sweetness and positive energy)
- A piece of parchment or paper and a pink or red pen (to write intentions)
- A quiet, comfortable space for the ritual
- A soft cloth or scarf (to create a comforting atmosphere)
- A journal or notebook (to record reflections)

Timing the Spell

The best time to perform this spell is on a Friday, the day ruled by Venus, which enhances love, comfort, and emotional healing. For added potency, perform the spell during a waxing moon, when the moon's energy supports growth, self-care, and the strengthening of positive emotions. The evening is a suitable time, as it allows you to unwind from the day and sink into a space of self-nurturing and relaxation.

Steps for the Emotional Healing Spell

1. Preparing the Sacred Space

Begin by selecting a quiet, comfortable space where you will not be disturbed. Spread the soft cloth or scarf on a surface in front of you, creating a gentle and comforting atmosphere. Set up the pink candle in the center, symbolizing Venus's nurturing energy. Arrange the honey, sweet foods, rose petals (or rose essential oil), sugar, and parchment around the candle.

Light the pink candle, focusing on its warm, gentle glow. Visualize the candlelight expanding, filling the space with a soothing pink aura that represents the loving, healing energy of Venus.

2. Setting Your Intentions for Healing

Close your eyes and take several deep breaths, inhaling calmness and exhaling any tension or emotional pain. Hold the intention in your mind that you are here to nurture and heal your emotional self. Bring to mind any emotions, situations, or memories that have been causing you distress or imbalance.

Take the piece of parchment and the pink or red pen. Write down your intentions for this spell. For example, you might write: "I release pain and welcome sweetness into my heart" or "I nurture myself with love, comfort, and care." Write from the heart, focusing on what you need for emotional healing.

When you have finished writing, fold the parchment and place it under the bowl of honey to infuse it with your intentions during the ritual.

3. Invoking the Energy of Venus

Sprinkle the rose petals around the bowl of honey or anoint the candle's base with rose essential oil, saying:

"Venus, goddess of love and grace, fill this space with your warm embrace. Let sweetness soothe, let love prevail, mend my heart and lift the veil."

Visualize a soft, pink light emanating from the candle and surrounding you, creating a cocoon of warmth and comfort. This is Venus's loving energy, enveloping you in a healing embrace.

4. The Sweetness of Honey: Anointing for Healing

Take the bowl of honey and dip your finger into it. Gently touch the honey to your heart chakra (the center of your chest) and say:

"Honey of gold, sweet and pure, heal my heart, let love endure. With this sweetness, pain dissolves, in Venus's light, my soul evolves."

As you anoint your heart with the honey, feel its warmth spreading through your chest, melting away any emotional pain or tension. Allow yourself to bask in the sensation of sweetness and self-love, letting it fill every corner of your being.

5. Eating the Sweet Foods for Emotional Comfort

Choose one of the sweet foods you have prepared and hold it in your hands. Before taking a bite, focus on its texture, color, and aroma. This food represents the sweetness of life and the comfort you deserve. As you bring the food to your lips, say:

"Sweetness of life, comfort I take, nourish my spirit, let love awake. As I eat, I am whole, love and warmth fill my soul."

Slowly eat the food, savoring each bite. As you chew, imagine the sweetness infusing your body with healing energy, spreading through every part of you and replacing sadness, worry, or pain with warmth and joy. Take your time, enjoying the experience of indulging in this small, comforting act of self-care.

6. Sealing the Spell with Sugar

After finishing the sweet food, take the dish of sugar and sprinkle a small amount over the parchment and honey, saying:

"Sugar of light, sweet and clear, seal this spell, bring love near. Let comfort stay, let healing be, sweetness within, so mote it be."

Visualize the sugar crystals glowing with a soft light, sealing in the energy of the spell and solidifying the warmth and comfort you have invoked.

7. Closing the Ritual

Spend a few moments sitting in the warmth of the candle's glow, feeling the effects of the spell settling into your body and heart. When you are ready, blow out the candle, allowing its smoke to carry your intentions for emotional healing and comfort to the universe.

As you extinguish the flame, say:

"By Venus's light, by honey's balm, I am healed, my heart is calm. Sweetness within, comfort surrounds, love and peace in me abounds."

Keep the parchment and honey in a special place, such as on your altar or bedside table, to continue infusing your space with the spell's energy.

8. Reflecting on the Ritual

After completing the spell, take a few moments to sit quietly and observe how you feel. Notice any sensations of warmth, relief, or newfound comfort. Open your journal and write down your experience, including the intentions you set, how you felt during the ritual, and any insights or emotions that arose.

Tips for Enhancing Emotional Healing

- **Repeat as Needed:** This spell can be performed whenever you feel the need for emotional healing and comfort. The more you engage with its energy, the stronger its effects will become.
- **Daily Honey Ritual:** Each morning, dip your finger into honey and touch your heart chakra, reciting a short affirmation like, "I embrace the sweetness of life and nurture myself with love."
- **Use Sweet Foods for Self-Care:** Incorporate sweet foods into your self-care routine, such as enjoying a piece of fruit or a small treat mindfully, to remind yourself of the spell's energy.

Final Thoughts

The "Sweet Balance: Emotional Healing Spell" is a gentle yet powerful way to nurture yourself and restore emotional harmony. By using the comforting qualities of sweet foods and honey, you tap into the energy of Venus to mend your heart, promote self-love, and create a space of warmth and self-care. This spell aligns with Libra's need for balance, allowing you to soothe emotional wounds and fill your life with the sweetness you deserve.

In moments of emotional turbulence, turning to the simple act of indulging in sweetness can provide a profound sense of comfort and healing. By combining this sensory experience with the magic of Venusian energy, you not only address the wounds of the heart but also nurture your spirit, reinforcing the idea that you are worthy of love, care, and joy. As you continue to work with this spell, let the sweetness of life remind you of your inner strength and the beauty that resides within you.

Chapter 16: The Scale's Shield: Protection Ritual

Libras, who are constantly seeking harmony, can often feel unbalanced when confronted with negative energies or difficult environments. Their natural sensitivity and empathy can leave them vulnerable to emotional disturbances, stress, and external negativity. "The Scale's Shield: Protection Ritual" is designed to create a protective barrier around oneself or a loved one, using the stabilizing power of crystals. This ritual draws upon Libra's natural affinity for balance and harmony, forging a shield that safeguards the energy field from unwanted influences while reinforcing inner peace and strength.

Crystals are renowned for their vibrational properties, which can be harnessed to create a shield of energy that acts as both a filter and a barrier against negativity. By aligning the crystals with your intention and using them in a focused ritual, you can erect an energetic shield that maintains the balance and serenity Libras thrive on. This ritual provides not only a method for immediate protection but also a way to strengthen one's resilience over time.

Selecting Protective Crystals for the Ritual

Certain crystals are particularly effective for protection, each resonating with different aspects of security and balance. For this ritual, you will work with a combination of crystals that provide grounding, protection, and emotional stability:

- **Black Tourmaline:** Known for its powerful protective qualities, black tourmaline absorbs and repels negative energy, grounding and shielding the aura.
- **Amethyst:** A calming stone that purifies the mind and spirit, amethyst aids in maintaining emotional balance while blocking negative influences.
- **Clear Quartz:** Amplifies the power of other crystals and seals the protective shield with clarity and light.

- **Rose Quartz:** Although primarily a stone of love, rose quartz adds a layer of gentle protection by promoting self-love and harmony, reinforcing the strength of the shield from within.
- **Selenite:** A high-vibrational stone that cleanses the aura and raises its frequency, creating a barrier that prevents negativity from penetrating.

Materials Needed

- One piece each of the following crystals: black tourmaline, amethyst, clear quartz, rose quartz, and selenite
- A white candle (to represent purity and light)
- A small bowl of salt water (for cleansing)
- A small pouch or cloth bag (to hold the crystals for a portable shield)
- A flat surface (like a table or altar) for creating the shield grid
- A piece of parchment or paper and a pen (to write protective affirmations)
- A quiet, undisturbed space for the ritual
- A journal or notebook (to record reflections)

Timing the Ritual

This ritual is best performed during a waning moon, a phase that supports release, protection, and the banishment of unwanted energies. For added potency, conduct the ritual on a Saturday, ruled by Saturn, the planet associated with boundaries, structure, and protection. You can perform this ritual at any time of day, but twilight is particularly effective as it marks the transition between day and night, symbolizing the creation of a protective boundary.

Steps for the Protection Ritual
1. Preparing the Sacred Space

Begin by choosing a quiet, comfortable space where you can perform the ritual undisturbed. Place the white candle in the center of your workspace, with the crystals arranged around it. Light the candle, allowing its flame to illuminate the space and create a circle of light and protection.

Take the bowl of salt water and dip each crystal into it one at a time, cleansing them of any residual energy they may have absorbed. As you cleanse each crystal, say:

"Crystal of [name], pure and clear, I cleanse you now to shield and steer."

After cleansing the crystals, place them on a flat surface to create a protective crystal grid in a circular shape. The black tourmaline should be at the bottom (south), amethyst at the top (north), clear quartz to the right (east), rose quartz to the left (west), and selenite in the center.

2. Setting Your Protective Intentions

Close your eyes and take a few deep breaths, inhaling calmness and exhaling any tension. Bring to mind the reason for creating this protective shield. It could be to protect yourself from negative energy, to help a loved one feel safe, or to safeguard your home environment. Visualize the desired outcome—see yourself or your loved one surrounded by a shimmering, impenetrable shield of light.

Take the piece of parchment and the pen. Write down your intentions for this ritual, such as: "I create a shield of protection, keeping negativity at bay and surrounding myself with peace and harmony." Be specific about the kind of protection you seek and what you wish to keep out of your energy field.

Fold the parchment and place it beneath the selenite crystal at the center of the grid. This action anchors your intention within the shield and aligns it with the crystals' energy.

3. Creating the Crystal Shield

Begin by focusing on the black tourmaline. This stone serves as the foundation of your protective shield, absorbing and repelling negativity. Hold the tourmaline in your hands and say:

"Black tourmaline, shield of might, absorb the dark, repel the blight. Ground my energy, keep me strong, protect my space, where I belong."

Place the black tourmaline back in its position at the bottom of the circle. Visualize a line of black light extending from the stone, forming the base of the protective shield.

Next, pick up the amethyst, which adds a layer of calm and spiritual protection to the shield. Hold the amethyst in your hands and say:

"Amethyst of violet light, calm my mind, guard me bright. Clear the space of negative flow, surround me now with peaceful glow."

Place the amethyst at the top of the circle, visualizing a purple light extending outward to form the top of the shield.

Now, take the clear quartz, which amplifies and seals the shield's energy. Hold the clear quartz and say:

"Clear quartz of power, crystal of light, amplify this shield, make it airtight. Protect with clarity, pure and strong, keep out what does not belong."

Place the clear quartz to the right of the circle, envisioning a clear, radiant light spreading across the entire shield, sealing it with clarity.

Next, hold the rose quartz in your hands. This stone adds a gentle, loving energy to the shield, protecting not just from external harm but also from internal negativity. Say:

"Rose quartz, love's warm embrace, shield with kindness, fill this space. Let harmony guard, let love be near, create this shield both strong and clear."

Place the rose quartz to the left of the circle, visualizing a soft pink light enveloping the shield, making it impenetrable yet compassionate.

Finally, pick up the selenite, the stone that cleanses and elevates the shield's vibration. Hold the selenite and say:

"Selenite of cleansing light, raise this shield to its height. Clear all darkness, keep it pure, this shield I create, strong and sure."

Place the selenite back in the center, over the folded parchment. Visualize a column of white light extending from the selenite upward, connecting with the other stones and completing the protective shield.

4. Sealing the Shield

Focus on the candle's flame and envision its light expanding outward, surrounding the entire crystal grid. See the light forming a dome-like shield around you (or the person you are protecting), shimmering with the combined energy of the crystals.

Say the following incantation to seal the shield:

"By earth and crystal, by light and might, I create this shield, strong and bright. No harm may enter, no darkness stay, protected I am, night and day. So mote it be."

Visualize the shield solidifying, its surface gleaming and pulsating with energy. Trust that it will now guard against negativity and maintain a space of harmony and balance.

5. Creating a Portable Shield Charm

Gather the crystals and place them into the small pouch or cloth bag. This charm can be carried with you or kept in a loved one's personal space to serve as a portable version of the protective shield you have created.

Hold the pouch close to your heart and say:

"Within this charm, my shield resides, protection strong, wherever it hides. By the power of crystal, my guard shall stay, keeping harm and darkness at bay."

Visualize the pouch glowing softly, filled with the shield's protective energy.

6. Closing the Ritual

To close the ritual, blow out the candle, allowing its smoke to carry your intention for protection to the universe. As you extinguish the flame, say:

"By candle's light and crystal's power, my shield is set, from this hour. Strong and true, it guards my way, in balance and peace, both night and day."

Keep the crystal pouch with you or place it in a loved one's space for ongoing protection. If you leave the grid in place, arrange it in a location where it will not be disturbed, allowing the shield's energy to remain active.

7. Reflecting on the Ritual

After completing the ritual, take a few moments to sit quietly and observe how you feel. Write down your experiences and any sensations of protection, peace, or strength you sensed during the ritual. Return to your journal in the future to reflect on how the protective shield has influenced your emotional and energetic state.

Tips for Maintaining and Enhancing the Shield

- **Recharge the Crystals:** Periodically cleanse and recharge the crystals, especially during the full moon, to maintain the shield's strength.
- **Daily Visualization:** Hold the pouch each morning and visualize the protective shield around you, reinforcing its energy.
- **Refresh the Ritual:** Perform this ritual whenever you feel the need to strengthen your protection or after encountering particularly draining situations.

Final Thoughts

"The Scale's Shield: Protection Ritual" is a powerful and nurturing way to guard your energy and create a harmonious space around you. By utilizing the balancing power of crystals and setting clear intentions, you forge a shield that protects against negativity and promotes inner peace. This ritual resonates with Libra's desire for balance and safety, ensuring that you or your loved one can navigate the world with confidence and serenity.

Remember, the shield you create is not just a barrier against harm but also a container for the harmonious energy you cultivate within. As you carry this protection with you, let it serve as a reminder of your strength, balance, and the loving energy that surrounds you.

Chapter 17: Wind's Whisper: Communication Spell

Communication is the cornerstone of healthy relationships, and for Libras, who value harmony and balance in their interactions, clear and open communication is essential. However, misunderstandings, unspoken emotions, and difficult conversations can create barriers, leading to imbalances in relationships. "Wind's Whisper: Communication Spell" is designed to enhance communication in relationships by invoking the energy of the air element. As an air sign, Libra is naturally associated with mental clarity, expression, and the free flow of ideas, making air-themed elements the perfect medium for improving communication.

In magic, the air element represents intellect, communication, inspiration, and the exchange of thoughts. By incorporating air-themed elements into this spell—such as feathers, incense, and breath—you can harness the energy of the wind to clear away confusion, promote understanding, and encourage the smooth flow of conversation. This spell aims to open the channels of communication between you and others, fostering honesty, empathy, and mutual respect.

Air-Themed Elements for Communication

Air-themed elements, such as feathers, incense, and breath, carry the vibrational qualities of the air element. These elements are symbolic of the unseen forces that move through our lives, including thoughts, words, and ideas. By using them in spellwork, you can tap into the natural flow of communication and facilitate more meaningful connections.

- **Feathers:** Represent the lightness and freedom of thought, aiding in the gentle delivery of words and ideas.
- **Incense:** Used to purify the air, promote mental clarity, and invoke the presence of the air element.
- **Breath:** The most direct connection to the air element, breathwork is used to focus the mind, calm the emotions, and prepare the spirit for open communication.

Materials Needed

- A white or yellow candle (to symbolize clarity, intellect, and air energy)
- A feather (preferably white, gray, or blue to represent the air element)
- Incense (such as frankincense, lavender, or sandalwood) to purify the air
- A small bell or wind chime (to invoke the sound of wind)
- A piece of parchment or paper and a blue pen (to write intentions)
- A small bowl of water mixed with sea salt (for cleansing)
- A quiet, airy space where there is some natural airflow (like near an open window)
- A journal or notebook (to record reflections)

Timing the Spell

This spell is most effective when performed during a waxing moon, as the growing light of the moon supports new beginnings and the development of positive energy. For enhanced influence, perform the ritual on a Wednesday, the day ruled by Mercury, the planet of communication and intellect. The ideal time for this spell is during the morning or early afternoon, when the air is fresh and full of life, symbolizing the opening of new lines of communication.

Steps for the Communication Spell

1. Preparing the Sacred Space

Choose a quiet, comfortable area with good airflow. Ideally, perform the spell near an open window to invite the presence of the air element. Begin by cleansing the space with the bowl of saltwater, sprinkling a few drops around to purify the environment and clear away stagnant energy.

Set up the white or yellow candle in front of you, placing the feather, incense, bell or wind chime, and parchment nearby. Light the candle, focusing on its flame as a source of clarity and illumination. Let its light create an atmosphere of openness and honesty.

2. Setting Your Intentions for Communication

Close your eyes and take several deep breaths, inhaling slowly through your nose and exhaling through your mouth. Imagine the air flowing through your body, clearing away any tension or blockages that may hinder open communication. As you breathe, visualize the air filling you with a sense of calmness and mental clarity.

Take the piece of parchment and the blue pen. Write down your intentions for this spell, focusing on what you wish to improve in your communication. For example: "I speak with clarity and kindness," or "May honesty and understanding flow between us." Be specific about the nature of the communication you want to enhance, whether it's a conversation with a partner, a friend, or a family member.

When you have finished writing, fold the parchment and place it near the candle to absorb its light and energy.

3. Invoking the Energy of the Air Element

Light the incense and wave it gently in the air, allowing its smoke to swirl and dance around you. This smoke represents the presence of the air element, purifying the space and opening the channels for communication. As you move the incense, say:

"Air of wisdom, air of grace, cleanse this space, open the place. Let words flow true, let thoughts be clear, bring understanding, bring love near."

Visualize the smoke creating a bridge between you and the person with whom you wish to communicate, clearing away any misunderstandings or barriers that may have existed.

4. Holding the Feather for Open Communication

Pick up the feather and hold it in both hands. This feather represents the lightness and freedom of open communication. Close your eyes and take a few deep breaths, feeling the air moving in and out of your lungs. Imagine the air carrying your intentions, lifting them up to the universe and into the space between you and the person you wish to connect with.

Say the following incantation:

"Feather of air, light and free, carry my words, bring them to thee. Let my voice be soft, my thoughts be clear, bring forth truth, dispel all fear."

Visualize the feather glowing with a soft blue or white light, radiating a calm, open energy that promotes honest and kind communication. Imagine this light extending outward, forming a bridge of understanding between you and the person you are focusing on.

5. Activating the Wind's Whisper

Hold the feather up to your lips and whisper softly into it the words or messages you wish to convey. Speak as though you are directly addressing the person, expressing your thoughts, feelings, or desires with clarity and sincerity. This act symbolizes the sending of your message on the winds, to be received with openness and understanding.

After whispering your messages, gently blow on the feather, imagining your breath carrying these words on the air to their intended recipient. Visualize the air currents sweeping away any negativity or miscommunication, leaving only truth and harmony in their wake.

6. Sealing the Spell with Sound

Take the bell or wind chime and gently ring it. The sound represents the voice of the wind, carrying your intentions out into the universe. As the sound resonates through the air, say:

"By the wind's whisper, by sound so clear, open the channels, bring harmony near. Let words be heard, let hearts align, in truth and love, our voices entwine."

Allow the sound to fade naturally, trusting that it has carried your intentions for open communication into the energetic realm.

7. Sealing the Spell

Gently blow out the candle, allowing the smoke to rise as a final offering to the air element. As you extinguish the flame, say:

"By air's light and wind's embrace, I seal this spell with love and grace. Let clarity flow, let truth take flight, communication open, pure and bright. So mote it be."

Place the feather, parchment, and incense in a safe place, such as on your altar or near an open window, to keep the energy of the spell active.

8. Reflecting on the Ritual

Sit quietly for a few moments, feeling the air around you. Notice any sensations of lightness, clarity, or peace that may have arisen during the ritual. Open your journal and write down your experience, including the intentions you set, how you felt, and any insights or emotions that surfaced. Return to your journal in the future to reflect on how the spell has influenced your communication.

Tips for Enhancing Communication

- **Daily Breathwork:** Each morning, hold the feather and take a few deep breaths, repeating the affirmation, "I speak with clarity and kindness," to reinforce the spell's energy.
- **Use Incense in Conversations:** Light incense during important conversations to maintain the spell's influence, creating an atmosphere of calm and openness.
- **Refresh the Spell:** Perform this ritual periodically, especially before significant discussions, to keep the channels of communication clear and harmonious.

Final Thoughts

The "Wind's Whisper: Communication Spell" is a powerful yet gentle way to improve communication in relationships, using the air element's qualities of clarity, freedom, and flow. By invoking the energy of the wind through the use of feathers, incense, and breath, you align with Libra's natural strengths in diplomacy, empathy, and intellectual connection. This spell not only facilitates clearer dialogue but also promotes a deeper understanding and connection between you and others.

Remember, effective communication is not just about speaking clearly but also about listening with an open heart and mind. As you continue to work with the energy of this spell, let the wind's whisper guide your interactions, fostering conversations that are filled with honesty, compassion, and mutual respect. In this way, you create relationships that are balanced, harmonious, and reflective of your true Libran nature.

Chapter 18: Justice's Eye: Conflict Resolution Spell

As a Libra, ruled by Venus and symbolized by the scales of justice, you naturally seek balance, harmony, and peace in your relationships and surroundings. However, conflicts are an inevitable part of life and can disturb the equilibrium you strive for. "Justice's Eye: Conflict Resolution Spell" is designed to help restore peace and understanding, using incense and balance-promoting crystals to create an atmosphere of calm, clarity, and fairness. This spell aligns with Libra's innate qualities of diplomacy, empathy, and fairness, harnessing the energy of the air element to open pathways for resolution and mutual understanding.

Crystals and incense have been used for centuries in various cultures to create a sacred space, promote clarity, and enhance emotional healing. By incorporating these elements into your conflict resolution spell, you tap into their natural abilities to cleanse negative energies, soothe heightened emotions, and bring a sense of equilibrium to the situation. The purpose of this spell is to not only resolve conflicts but also to restore a sense of inner and outer peace, allowing all involved to move forward with renewed balance.

The Role of Crystals and Incense in Conflict Resolution

Certain crystals are known for their ability to promote balance, calmness, and harmony—qualities that are essential for resolving disputes. Similarly, incense represents the air element and is used to purify spaces, calm the mind, and facilitate open communication. This spell uses a combination of these tools to create an environment conducive to peaceful resolution.

- **Rose Quartz:** Promotes unconditional love, compassion, and forgiveness, helping to soothe emotions and open the heart to understanding.
- **Amethyst:** Brings calmness, spiritual insight, and emotional balance, aiding in clear and rational communication.

- **Blue Lace Agate:** Encourages gentle communication and clarity, making it easier to express one's thoughts and listen to others with empathy.
- **Clear Quartz:** Amplifies the energy of other crystals and promotes mental clarity, helping to see the situation objectively.
- **Incense:** Lavender, frankincense, or sandalwood incense is used to purify the space and calm heightened emotions.

Materials Needed

- Rose quartz, amethyst, blue lace agate, and clear quartz crystals
- Lavender, frankincense, or sandalwood incense (for purification and calming)
- A white or light blue candle (to symbolize peace, balance, and clarity)
- A small bowl of water mixed with sea salt (for cleansing)
- A piece of parchment or paper and a blue or white pen (to write intentions)
- A fireproof dish or incense holder
- A quiet, undisturbed space for the ritual
- A journal or notebook (to record reflections)

Timing the Spell

This spell is best performed during a waxing moon, when the moon's energy supports the growth of positive outcomes and new beginnings. If possible, perform the ritual on a Friday (ruled by Venus) to invoke the energies of love, harmony, and reconciliation. Alternatively, a Monday (ruled by the Moon) can aid in emotional clarity. The spell can be conducted at any time of day, but dusk is particularly effective as it symbolizes the closing of a day and the transition into a state of calm.

Steps for the Conflict Resolution Spell
1. Preparing the Sacred Space

Choose a quiet, comfortable area where you will not be disturbed. Begin by cleansing the space with the bowl of salt water, sprinkling a few drops around to purify the environment. This step clears away any lingering negative energy, creating a neutral ground for the conflict resolution to take place.

Set up the white or light blue candle in the center of your space, with the crystals arranged around it. Place the incense and its holder nearby, as well as the parchment and pen.

2. Setting Your Intentions for Resolution

Close your eyes and take a few deep breaths, inhaling calmness and exhaling tension. Bring the conflict to mind, focusing on your desire to resolve it peacefully and fairly. Imagine both parties finding common ground and moving forward with mutual understanding.

Take the piece of parchment and pen. Write down your intentions for this spell, such as: "May peace and understanding be restored," or "I seek a fair and harmonious resolution for all involved." Be specific and focus on the outcome you wish to achieve, emphasizing harmony, clarity, and balance.

Fold the parchment and place it near the candle, allowing it to absorb the light and energy as you perform the ritual.

3. Invoking Balance with Incense

Light the incense and wave it gently through the air, allowing the smoke to swirl around the space. This smoke represents the clearing away of tension and negativity, as well as the opening of pathways for peaceful communication. As you move the incense, say:

"Air of calm, smoke of light, clear the air, restore the right. Let peace descend, let hearts now hear, dissolve the conflict, dispel the fear."

Visualize the incense smoke carrying away the heaviness and confusion of the conflict, replacing it with a light, harmonious energy that invites resolution and mutual understanding.

4. Activating the Crystals for Peaceful Resolution

One by one, hold each crystal in your hands and set its specific intention:

- **Rose Quartz:** Hold the rose quartz and say: *"Rose quartz, stone of love, soften hearts, bring peace thereof. Let compassion flow, let wounds mend, open the path where peace extends."* Visualize a soft pink light radiating from the crystal, filling the space with warmth and understanding.
- **Amethyst:** Hold the amethyst and say: *"Amethyst of calm and mind, bring clarity, let truth be kind. Balance emotions, soothe the soul, make communication whole."* Picture a purple light emanating from the amethyst, calming emotions and promoting a balanced perspective.
- **Blue Lace Agate:** Hold the blue lace agate and say: *"Stone of words, gentle and clear, help us speak, help us hear, Let truth flow with calm embrace, bring peace to fill this space."* Envision a pale blue light radiating from the stone, facilitating honest yet compassionate dialogue.
- **Clear Quartz:** Hold the clear quartz and say: *"Clear quartz of light, amplify power, bring clarity to this hour. Let all see truth, let balance stay, clear the path, show the way."* Imagine a bright white light shining from the crystal, amplifying the intentions of harmony and resolution.

Place the crystals in a circular formation around the candle, creating a grid of balanced energy. See the lights from each crystal merging to form a unified, harmonious glow.

5. Lighting the Candle for Clarity

Light the white or light blue candle, focusing on its flame as a source of peace, clarity, and balance. As the flame burns, imagine it illuminating the situation, revealing the paths to understanding and reconciliation.

Say the following incantation:

"By candle's light and crystal's glow, let truth and peace between us flow. Dissolve the conflict, end the strife, restore the balance, heal our life. So mote it be."

Visualize the candle's light spreading outward, enveloping all parties involved in the conflict with warmth, understanding, and harmony.

6. Visualizing Resolution

Sit quietly and focus on the area around the candle and crystals. Picture the situation or the individuals involved in the conflict. Imagine a bridge of light forming between them, facilitating open, honest, and compassionate communication. Envision the tension dissolving and being replaced by mutual respect, empathy, and a desire for peace.

Hold this vision in your mind, allowing the energy of the crystals, candle, and incense to guide you. Trust that this spell is working to open the channels for resolution, promoting fairness and understanding on all sides.

7. Sealing the Spell

To seal the spell, extinguish the candle gently, allowing its smoke to carry your intention for peace and resolution into the universe. As you do so, say:

"By flame now quenched and air now still, peace restored by loving will. Balance returns, harmony stays, justice guides us in our ways. So mote it be."

Gather the crystals and place them into a pouch or on a personal altar to keep the energy of the spell active. Keep the folded parchment with the crystals as a reminder of your intention for resolution.

8. Reflecting on the Ritual

After completing the ritual, take a few moments to sit quietly and notice how you feel. Write down your experience in your journal, including the intentions you set, the emotions that surfaced, and any insights you received during the spell. In the days following, observe how the situation evolves and how communication and understanding unfold between the parties involved.

Tips for Maintaining Harmony

- **Daily Affirmations:** Hold the rose quartz each morning and recite a simple affirmation such as, "I embrace peace and harmony in my relationships," to reinforce the spell's energy.
- **Use Incense During Discussions:** Light incense before difficult conversations to maintain the spell's influence and create a calm, balanced environment.
- **Refresh the Spell:** Perform this ritual periodically, especially when facing new conflicts, to maintain a sense of harmony and open communication.

Final Thoughts

"Justice's Eye: Conflict Resolution Spell" is a powerful tool for restoring balance and peace in the face of conflict. By combining the energies of crystals and incense with clear intentions, you align with the Libran principles of diplomacy, fairness, and understanding. This spell not only addresses the immediate issue but also creates a foundation of harmony and mutual respect for the future.

Conflict resolution is not about winning or losing but about finding common ground and restoring equilibrium. As you work with this spell, allow it to guide you in navigating difficult situations with empathy, clarity, and a commitment to justice. In doing so, you embody the

Libran ideal of harmony, bringing light and balance into your relation-ships and your world.

Chapter 19: Golden Hour: Prosperity Spell

Prosperity, wealth, and abundance are qualities that resonate deeply with Libra's connection to Venus, the planet of beauty, love, and luxury. Libras naturally enjoy the finer things in life and strive for balance in all areas, including financial well-being. However, to achieve prosperity and maintain equilibrium in life, one often needs to align with the energies of abundance and open oneself to receiving the wealth the universe has to offer. The "Golden Hour: Prosperity Spell" is designed to attract wealth, success, and financial security using gold-colored candles, herbs, and crystals. This spell channels the energy of the golden hour—the magical time of day when the world is bathed in a warm, golden light—to invoke the feeling of abundance and prosperity.

In magical practices, gold symbolizes wealth, luxury, and the radiant light of the sun, which is often associated with success and growth. By using gold-colored candles and herbs in this spell, you tap into the vibrational frequency of abundance, inviting prosperity into your life. The ritual combines the energies of light, warmth, and growth to create a powerful magnetic force that draws wealth and opportunities toward you.

Gold-Colored Candles and Prosperity Herbs

Gold-colored candles serve as the focal point of this spell, representing the light, warmth, and wealth of the sun. Herbs, on the other hand, have been used for centuries in prosperity magic due to their natural properties of attraction and abundance. Here's how they contribute to the prosperity spell:

- **Gold Candle:** Symbolizes wealth, luxury, success, and the radiant light of abundance. Lighting a gold candle creates a beacon that draws prosperity and wealth.
- **Herbs:**
    - **Basil:** A potent herb for attracting wealth, success, and luck. It promotes financial stability and encourages growth.
    - **Cinnamon:** Associated with money, protection, and speed, cinnamon accelerates the flow of prosperity into your life.
    - **Bay Leaf:** Used in spells for manifestation and success, bay leaves amplify intentions and attract opportunities.
    - **Chamomile:** Promotes calmness and peace, helping to clear financial worries and create a welcoming space for abundance.

Materials Needed

- A gold-colored candle (to represent wealth, abundance, and success)
- A small dish of herbs: basil, cinnamon, bay leaves, and chamomile
- A piece of pyrite (also known as fool's gold) or citrine crystal (for attracting wealth and prosperity)
- A small bowl of sea salt (for purification)
- A gold or yellow cloth (to create a sacred space)

- A piece of parchment or paper and a gold or green pen (to write intentions)
- A lighter or matches
- A small dish (for burning the bay leaves)
- A quiet, comfortable space for the ritual
- A journal or notebook (to record reflections)

Timing the Spell

This spell is best performed during a waxing moon, when the moon's energy supports growth, manifestation, and the attraction of abundance. For added potency, conduct the ritual on a Sunday, ruled by the sun, or a Thursday, ruled by Jupiter, the planet of expansion and prosperity. The ideal time for the spell is during the golden hour—sunrise or sunset—when the world is bathed in a warm, golden light, symbolizing the energy of abundance.

Steps for the Prosperity Spell

1. Preparing the Sacred Space

Choose a quiet, comfortable area for the ritual. Begin by cleansing the space with the bowl of sea salt, sprinkling a few grains around to purify the environment and clear away any lingering negative energy that may block prosperity. Spread the gold or yellow cloth on a flat surface to create a sacred space where the spell will be performed.

Arrange the gold candle, herbs, pyrite or citrine crystal, parchment, and pen on the cloth. Place the small dish for burning bay leaves nearby, along with the lighter or matches.

2. Setting Your Intentions for Prosperity

Close your eyes and take several deep breaths, inhaling feelings of calmness and exhaling any stress or worry related to finances. Visualize golden light surrounding you, filling your entire being with warmth, confidence, and the energy of abundance. Bring to mind the kind of prosperity you seek—whether it's financial gain, career success, or an influx of opportunities.

Take the parchment and the gold or green pen. Write down your intentions for the spell. Be specific about what you desire, such as "I attract financial abundance," or "I am open to receiving wealth and opportunities in all forms." Focus on the feeling of already having this prosperity in your life, allowing gratitude and positivity to fill your heart.

When you have finished writing, fold the parchment and place it under the gold candle, allowing it to absorb the candle's energy during the ritual.

3. Creating the Prosperity Circle with Herbs

In the small dish, mix the basil, cinnamon, and chamomile together. Take a pinch of the mixture and sprinkle it in a circle around the candle, saying:

"Herbs of wealth, herbs of light, draw abundance, shining bright. By basil's growth, by cinnamon's fire, by chamomile's peace, bring forth my desire."

As you sprinkle the herbs, visualize each grain radiating golden light, forming a circle of abundance around you and the candle. This circle represents the flow of prosperity that you are inviting into your life.

4. Lighting the Gold Candle for Abundance

Light the gold candle, focusing on its flame as a beacon of wealth and success. As the candle burns, visualize its light growing brighter, reaching out to the universe and drawing prosperity toward you.

Say the following incantation:

"Golden flame, wealth's warm glow, attract abundance, let it flow. Success and fortune, come to me, in golden light, so mote it be."

Imagine the flame expanding, filling the room with its golden light, and creating a magnetic field that attracts wealth and opportunities into your life.

5. Burning the Bay Leaves for Manifestation

Take a bay leaf and hold it in your hands. Focus on your intentions for prosperity, imagining them already manifesting in your life. Visualize the bay leaf absorbing this energy and transforming it into a symbol of your desire.

Light the bay leaf using the candle's flame and place it in the dish to burn. As the bay leaf burns, say:

"Bay leaf of power, bay leaf of might, transform my wish, make it right. As you burn, my wealth does grow, prosperity flows, in sun's warm glow."

Watch as the smoke rises, carrying your intentions for abundance into the universe. Trust that your desires are being heard and that the energy of the bay leaf is amplifying your call for prosperity.

6. Charging the Crystal

Pick up the pyrite or citrine crystal and hold it in your hands. Close your eyes and visualize the crystal glowing with golden light. Imagine it absorbing the energy of the candle and herbs, becoming a magnet for wealth and success.

Say:

"Crystal of wealth, crystal of gain, draw prosperity, remove all strain. Hold my desire, shine so bright, bring fortune's favor into my sight."

Place the charged crystal beside the candle, allowing it to continue absorbing the candle's energy as it burns.

7. Sealing the Spell

To seal the spell, blow out the candle gently, sending a final puff of golden light into the universe. As you extinguish the flame, say:

"By golden light and herb's sweet power, I seal this spell in fortune's hour. Wealth and abundance now come to me, as I will it, so mote it be."

Keep the parchment and crystal in a special place, such as on your altar or in a prosperity jar, to maintain the spell's influence. The crystal will serve as a talisman, attracting wealth and abundance wherever it is kept.

8. Reflecting on the Ritual

After completing the ritual, take a few moments to sit quietly and notice how you feel. Open your journal and write down your experience, including the intentions you set, how you felt during the ritual, and any insights or emotions that arose. In the days and weeks following, observe how prosperity manifests in your life and how your financial situation begins to change.

Tips for Enhancing Prosperity

- **Daily Wealth Affirmations:** Hold the crystal each morning and recite a wealth affirmation, such as "I attract prosperity and success effortlessly," to reinforce the spell's energy.
- **Use the Herbs:** Sprinkle a small pinch of the herb mixture in your wallet or on your work desk to keep the energy of abundance around you.
- **Refresh the Spell:** Perform this ritual monthly, especially during the waxing moon, to keep the flow of prosperity strong and active in your life.

Final Thoughts

The "Golden Hour: Prosperity Spell" is a powerful ritual that harnesses the energy of gold and herbs to attract wealth, success, and abundance into your life. By aligning with the warmth and radiance of the golden hour, you open yourself to the universe's gifts and welcome prosperity with gratitude and confidence. This spell resonates with Libra's love for balance, beauty, and luxury, allowing you to manifest financial stability and opportunities while maintaining harmony in all areas of your life.

Prosperity is more than just financial gain; it is about cultivating a mindset of abundance, where you are open to receiving and sharing the wealth that flows into your life. As you work with this spell, let its energy remind you of the golden light that resides within you—a light that attracts success, prosperity, and all the joys of a life lived in balance.

Chapter 20: Harmony in the Home: Domestic Peace Spell

Libras thrive in environments that are balanced, beautiful, and harmonious. The home is a sanctuary where they can unwind, recharge, and find comfort. However, when the atmosphere in the home becomes chaotic due to stress, disagreements, or negative energies, it can disrupt the sense of peace that Libras so deeply cherish. "Harmony in the Home: Domestic Peace Spell" is designed to create a serene and loving environment using specific scents and charms. This spell draws on the calming and balancing energies of nature to cleanse, harmonize, and infuse your living space with tranquility and positivity.

Scents have long been used in various cultures to promote relaxation, cleanse negative energies, and invoke specific moods. Combined with charms—small objects imbued with magical intent—they can become powerful tools for cultivating an atmosphere of peace and harmony. By using these elements, this spell allows you to transform your home into a haven of balance, comfort, and joy.

Scents and Charms for Domestic Peace

Certain scents have the power to soothe the mind, ease tensions, and promote feelings of love and harmony. Paired with charms that represent balance and protection, they create an energetic shield that keeps negativity at bay while encouraging positive interactions within the home.

- **Scents:**
  - **Lavender:** Known for its calming and soothing properties, lavender promotes relaxation, reduces stress, and invites harmony.
  - **Rose:** Represents love, beauty, and emotional balance. Rose scent helps to heal emotional wounds and foster compassion.
  - **Sandalwood:** Used to ground and purify energy, sandalwood encourages a peaceful and balanced atmosphere.

- **Charms:**
  - **Rose Quartz:** A crystal that symbolizes unconditional love and emotional healing, encouraging kindness and understanding in the household.
  - **Amethyst:** Promotes calmness, emotional balance, and spiritual protection, helping to maintain a serene atmosphere.
  - **Small Bells:** The gentle sound of bells is believed to disperse negative energy and attract positive vibes, ensuring that harmony prevails.

Materials Needed

- Lavender, rose, and sandalwood essential oils (or incense if oils are unavailable)
- A small spray bottle filled with distilled water (to create a scented room spray)
- Rose quartz and amethyst crystals
- A small charm bag (preferably pink or white)
- Small bells (to hang around the home)
- A piece of parchment or paper and a pink pen (to write your intentions)
- A white candle (to symbolize purity, peace, and harmony)
- A lighter or matches
- A quiet, comfortable space for the ritual
- A journal or notebook (to record reflections)

Timing the Spell

This spell is best performed during a waxing moon, which supports growth, positivity, and the strengthening of harmonious energies. For added effectiveness, perform the spell on a Friday, ruled by Venus, the planet of love, beauty, and balance. Conduct the ritual in the evening when the day's activities have wound down, symbolizing the creation of a peaceful space for rest and relaxation.

Steps for the Domestic Peace Spell
1. Preparing the Sacred Space

Choose a quiet and comfortable area of your home to perform the ritual. Begin by setting up a small altar with the white candle, essential oils, crystals, charm bag, and bells. Light the candle, focusing on its flame as a symbol of purity and peace that you wish to infuse into your living space.

Take a few moments to center yourself. Close your eyes, take several deep breaths, and envision a peaceful and loving atmosphere surrounding you. As you exhale, release any tension or stress, allowing yourself to become fully present in the moment.

2. Creating the Scented Spray for Harmony

Combine a few drops of lavender, rose, and sandalwood essential oils into the spray bottle filled with distilled water. As you add each drop, visualize its properties filling the water with calming, loving, and grounding energy. Say the following words:

- For Lavender: *"Lavender, calm and pure, bring peace, make harmony endure."*
- For Rose: *"Rose of love, warm and sweet, let hearts be kind in every beat."*
- For Sandalwood: *"Sandalwood of grounding light, purify my home, make it right."*

Secure the lid on the bottle and gently shake it, mixing the scents together. This spray will serve as a fragrant mist to cleanse and harmonize the energy within your home.

3. Infusing the Crystals with Peaceful Intentions

Hold the rose quartz crystal in your hands and close your eyes. Visualize it glowing with a soft pink light, representing unconditional love and emotional harmony. Say:

"Rose quartz of love and peace, bring warmth to my home, let tension cease. Fill each room with kindness bright, make love and joy take flight."

Next, hold the amethyst crystal. Picture it radiating a calming purple light, absorbing any negativity and transforming it into tranquility. Say:

"Amethyst of calm and grace, protect this home, hold sacred space. Balance emotions, keep us clear, let peace and comfort dwell here."

Place both crystals into the charm bag, allowing their energies to blend and create a continuous source of harmony within the household.

4. Charging the Bells for Protection and Harmony

Take the small bells and hold them in your hands. Visualize their sound vibrating throughout your home, dispersing negativity and inviting positive, peaceful energies. As you hold the bells, say:

"Bells of harmony, sound so clear, bring joy and peace to all who hear. Dispel the darkness, fill with light, make this home calm, warm, and bright."

Hang the bells near the entrances of your home, such as the front door or windows. This will create a barrier that repels negativity and allows only harmonious energy to enter.

5. Writing Your Intentions for Domestic Peace

Take the piece of parchment and the pink pen. Write down your intentions for the spell, such as: "May this home be filled with peace, love, and understanding," or "Let harmony and joy dwell in every room, bringing comfort to all who live here." Write from the heart, focusing on the atmosphere you wish to create within your living space.

Fold the parchment and place it inside the charm bag with the crystals, sealing your intentions within the bag.

6. Using the Scented Spray

Take the scented spray and gently spritz it around the room, focusing on corners, doorways, and areas where tension may accumulate. As you spray, say:

"Mists of peace, scents so light, cleanse this space, make it bright. Fill each corner, every wall, bring calm and love to one and all."

Visualize the mist filling the room with a soft, glowing light that settles over every surface, purifying the energy and leaving behind an aura of serenity.

7. Sealing the Spell

To seal the spell, hold the charm bag in your hands and close your eyes. Visualize the bag glowing with a warm, radiant light, emanating peace and harmony throughout your home. Say:

"By crystal's light and scent's embrace, I seal this spell in time and space. Let peace remain, let love now flow, harmony reigns, as I will it so. So mote it be."

Place the charm bag in a central location within your home, such as on your altar, mantle, or a special shelf. This will act as a constant source of peace and harmony in your living space.

8. Reflecting on the Ritual

Sit quietly for a few moments and notice how the atmosphere in your home feels. Open your journal and write down your experience, including your intentions, the scents you used, and any sensations or emotions you felt during the ritual. In the days and weeks following, observe how the energy in your home changes and how it affects the interactions among its inhabitants.

Tips for Maintaining Domestic Harmony

- **Daily Spritz:** Use the scented spray daily or whenever you feel tension building up in the home to maintain a serene atmosphere.
- **Ring the Bells:** Ring the bells near your doorways occasionally to refresh the protective and harmonious energy.
- **Cleanse Crystals:** Periodically cleanse the crystals in the charm bag by placing them under the moonlight or washing them in saltwater to recharge their energy.

Final Thoughts

The "Harmony in the Home: Domestic Peace Spell" is a gentle yet powerful way to create a loving, peaceful, and balanced environment within your living space. By combining the energies of scents and charms, you invoke the calming and harmonizing qualities of nature, transforming your home into a sanctuary of comfort and positivity. This spell resonates with Libra's desire for beauty and balance, ensuring that the home remains a place of refuge and joy.

Remember, a harmonious home is not only a space free of conflict but also one that nurtures and uplifts all who dwell within it. As you work with this spell, let its energy remind you to approach your living environment with love, care, and an open heart, creating a ripple effect of peace that extends beyond the walls of your home.

Chapter 21: Venusian Affection: Friendship Bonding Spell

Friendships are essential for Libras, who deeply value their connections and seek harmonious relationships. Ruled by Venus, the planet of love, beauty, and social harmony, Libras possess a natural affinity for forming close bonds. However, even the strongest friendships require nurturing and strengthening over time. The "Venusian Affection: Friendship Bonding Spell" is designed to deepen the connection between friends, using a blend of Libra-associated herbs and crystals. This ritual calls upon the energy of Venus to enhance feelings of trust, loyalty, and affection, fostering a more profound sense of unity and understanding.

Herbs and crystals have long been used in magical practices for their specific vibrational properties. By selecting those that resonate with Libra's qualities of love, harmony, and balance, this spell creates a sacred space to celebrate friendship. The ritual blends these elements with intention, reinforcing the bond between friends and opening the way for continued growth, joy, and support in the relationship.

Libra's Herbs and Crystals for Friendship

Libra is associated with several herbs and crystals that promote love, harmony, and peace—key qualities for deepening friendships. Here's how each of these magical elements plays a role in this spell:

- **Herbs:**
  - **Rose:** Symbolizing love and emotional harmony, rose petals invite warmth, affection, and beauty into the friendship.
  - **Lavender:** Known for its calming and soothing properties, lavender promotes understanding, emotional support, and balance in relationships.

- ◦ **Thyme:** Represents courage, loyalty, and respect, essential components for building a strong friendship.
- ◦ **Catnip:** Encourages playfulness, joy, and companionship, infusing the relationship with light-hearted energy.
- **Crystals:**
  - ◦ **Rose Quartz:** The stone of unconditional love and friendship, rose quartz opens the heart to compassion, forgiveness, and deeper emotional bonds.
  - ◦ **Green Aventurine:** Encourages growth, optimism, and mutual support, promoting the flow of positive energy within the friendship.
  - ◦ **Amethyst:** Enhances spiritual connection, emotional balance, and communication, helping friends to better understand each other's feelings.

Materials Needed

- Rose petals, lavender, thyme, and catnip (dried or fresh)
- Rose quartz, green aventurine, and amethyst crystals
- A pink or green candle (to symbolize love, friendship, and harmony)
- A small bowl or dish (for mixing the herbs)
- A pink or green ribbon (to create a friendship charm)
- A small pouch or cloth bag (to hold the charm)
- A piece of parchment or paper and a pink or green pen (to write intentions)
- A lighter or matches
- A quiet, comfortable space for the ritual
- A journal or notebook (to record reflections)

Timing the Spell

The best time to perform this ritual is during a waxing moon, which supports the strengthening and growth of relationships. For added effectiveness, perform the spell on a Friday, the day ruled by Venus, to infuse the friendship with love, harmony, and beauty. The spell can be conducted at any time of day, but evening is particularly suitable as it represents a time for connection and reflection.

Steps for the Friendship Bonding Spell
1. Preparing the Sacred Space

Choose a quiet, comfortable space where you and your friend (or friends) can sit together without interruptions. Begin by setting up an altar or a small surface with the pink or green candle, herbs, crystals, ribbon, pouch, parchment, and pen. Light the candle, focusing on its flame as a symbol of warmth, love, and unity.

Take a moment to center yourself. Close your eyes, take several deep breaths, and visualize the bond between you and your friend(s) strengthening, glowing with a warm, pink light. Feel the sense of joy, trust, and connection that you share.

2. Mixing the Herb Blend for Friendship

In the small bowl or dish, combine the herbs: rose petals, lavender, thyme, and catnip. As you add each herb, focus on its unique properties and the qualities it brings to the friendship:

- **Rose:** *"Rose of love, warm and true, strengthen our bond, renew and imbue."*
- **Lavender:** *"Lavender of calm and grace, bring understanding, fill this space."*
- **Thyme:** *"Thyme of courage, loyalty deep, safeguard this friendship, in trust we keep."*
- **Catnip:** *"Catnip of joy, light and free, bring laughter and playfulness, so mote it be."*

Gently mix the herbs with your hands, visualizing them glowing with a gentle, pink light. Feel the energy of love, harmony, and joy infusing the blend, ready to nurture your friendship.

3. Infusing the Crystals with Friendship Energy

One by one, hold each crystal in your hands and set its specific intention for the friendship:

- **Rose Quartz:** Hold the rose quartz and say: *"Rose quartz, stone of love, open our hearts to compassion above. Let kindness flow, let joy remain, deepen our bond, free from pain."*
- **Green Aventurine:** Hold the green aventurine and say: *"Aventurine of growth and care, bring us support, in life to share. Let optimism guide our way, in friendship strong, come what may."*
- **Amethyst:** Hold the amethyst and say: *"Amethyst of balance and light, enhance our bond, keep it right. Clear our minds, our spirits align, in harmony true, our friendship shines."*

Place the crystals into the center of the herb blend, allowing their energies to mix and amplify the spell's intention.

4. Creating the Friendship Charm

Cut a length of the pink or green ribbon and tie it into a loose knot. As you do so, say:

"Ribbon of love, ribbon of light, weave us together, strong and tight. By this charm, our bond is sealed, in joy and trust, our friendship healed."

Sprinkle a pinch of the herb blend onto the ribbon, visualizing the energy of the herbs and crystals infusing the charm with warmth, love, and harmony.

5. Writing Intentions for Friendship

Take the piece of parchment and the pen. Write down your intentions for the friendship, such as: "May our friendship be filled with love, joy, and mutual support," or "Let our bond grow stronger with each passing day, in harmony and trust." Be specific and heartfelt in your words, focusing on the qualities you wish to enhance within your relationship.

Fold the parchment and place it into the pouch. Add the ribbon charm and the crystals, then sprinkle the remaining herbs into the pouch. Draw the pouch closed, holding it in your hands as you close your eyes and focus on your intentions.

6. Sealing the Spell

To seal the spell, hold the pouch in front of the candle and say:

"By Venus's grace and love so true, I seal this charm, for me and you. Let friendship grow, let hearts now blend, in trust and joy, until the end. So mote it be."

Visualize a warm, pink light emanating from the candle, surrounding the pouch and sealing the energies within. Feel the power of love, joy, and unity radiating from the charm, strengthening the bond between you and your friend(s).

7. Sharing the Charm

After the ritual, give the pouch to your friend as a token of your bond and a reminder of the love and harmony you share. Encourage them to keep the charm in a special place, such as on their bedside table, in a drawer, or in their bag, to carry the spell's energy with them.

8. Reflecting on the Ritual

Sit quietly for a few moments and reflect on the experience. Open your journal and write down your feelings, the intentions you set, and any emotions or insights that arose during the ritual. In the days and weeks following, observe how the energy of the spell influences your friendship and how the bond deepens.

Tips for Maintaining a Strong Friendship

- **Daily Affirmations:** Hold the rose quartz and repeat a simple affirmation like, "Our friendship grows stronger every day," to keep the bond's energy vibrant.
- **Regular Charm Cleansing:** Cleanse the crystals periodically by placing the charm under moonlight or sprinkling it with a bit of lavender water to recharge its energy.

- **Plan Rituals Together:** To further strengthen your bond, consider performing this spell or other bonding rituals together on a regular basis.

Final Thoughts

"Venusian Affection: Friendship Bonding Spell" is a heartwarming and powerful way to honor and deepen the connection you share with a friend. By using a blend of Libra's herbs and crystals, you draw upon the energy of Venus to infuse your friendship with love, harmony, and joy. This spell aligns perfectly with Libra's desire for balanced and meaningful relationships, helping to foster a space of mutual support, understanding, and lasting affection.

Friendship is a precious gift that requires care, attention, and nurturing to flourish. As you work with the energy of this spell, let it remind you of the beauty and strength that comes from a bond built on trust, love, and shared experiences. Embrace the light of Venus, and let it guide your friendship toward a future filled with joy, harmony, and lasting affection.

Chapter 22: Balance of Hearts: Love Spell

Libras are known for their romantic nature, seeking deep, balanced connections in their relationships. Ruled by Venus, the planet of love, beauty, and harmony, Libras are natural romantics who strive for fairness and equality in their partnerships. The "Balance of Hearts: Love Spell" is crafted to either attract a new romantic love that aligns with your energy or strengthen an existing relationship by infusing it with balance, harmony, and mutual respect. This spell focuses on creating a love that reflects the essence of Libra: passionate yet balanced, emotional yet rational, and tender yet strong.

The key to a successful love spell lies in the intention behind it. This spell does not seek to force feelings or manipulate emotions but rather to attract the kind of love that will complement and uplift both partners. It is designed to enhance the qualities of mutual respect, understanding, and affection that are essential for a balanced and harmonious partnership. Through the use of carefully selected herbs, crystals, and ritual elements, this spell harnesses the energy of Venus to help create a love that is both fulfilling and enduring.

Herbs and Crystals for Love, Balance, and Harmony

Herbs and crystals have been used in love spells for centuries due to their natural properties of attraction, love, and emotional balance. The ones chosen for this spell are particularly attuned to Libra's need for harmony and equality in relationships:

- **Herbs:**
    - **Rose:** The quintessential herb of love, roses symbolize beauty, passion, and affection. Rose petals attract loving energy and help cultivate deep emotional connections.
    - **Jasmine:** Enhances spiritual love, romance, and emotional intimacy, fostering a deep connection between partners.

- **Lavender:** Promotes calmness, balance, and a sense of peace in romantic relationships, helping to ease tensions and open the heart to love.
- **Basil:** Attracts love, fidelity, and trust, ensuring that relationships are founded on mutual respect and honesty.
- **Crystals:**
  - **Rose Quartz:** The stone of unconditional love, it opens the heart chakra, allowing for the flow of love, compassion, and emotional healing.
  - **Green Aventurine:** Encourages emotional stability, optimism, and balance, creating an environment where love can thrive.
  - **Amethyst:** Enhances emotional clarity, spiritual connection, and understanding between partners.

Materials Needed

- Rose petals, jasmine flowers, lavender, and basil (dried or fresh)
- Rose quartz, green aventurine, and amethyst crystals
- A pink or red candle (to symbolize love, passion, and harmony)
- A small bowl or dish (for mixing the herbs)
- A piece of parchment or paper and a pink or red pen (to write intentions)
- A pink or red ribbon (to create a love charm)
- A small pouch or cloth bag (to hold the charm)
- A small bowl of sea salt (for purification)
- A lighter or matches
- A quiet, comfortable space for the ritual
- A journal or notebook (to record reflections)

Timing the Spell

The best time to perform this love spell is during a waxing or full moon, when the moon's energy is at its peak for attracting love and enhancing emotional bonds. For added potency, perform the spell on a Friday, the day ruled by Venus, to align with the energies of love, beauty, and harmony. The ideal time is in the evening, when the atmosphere is naturally more romantic and calm, providing the perfect setting for connecting with your heart's desires.

Steps for the Love Spell

1. Preparing the Sacred Space

Select a quiet, comfortable area where you can perform the ritual without disturbance. Begin by cleansing the space with sea salt, sprinkling a few grains around to purify the environment and clear away any negative energy that might block the flow of love. Place the pink or red candle at the center of your ritual space, with the herbs, crystals, ribbon, pouch, parchment, and pen arranged around it.

Light the candle, focusing on its soft, warm glow as a beacon of love, warmth, and harmony. Allow its light to fill the space, creating an atmosphere of openness and romance.

2. Setting Your Intentions for Love

Close your eyes and take several deep breaths, inhaling feelings of love, warmth, and serenity. As you exhale, release any tension or doubts that may hinder your intention for love. Visualize your heart surrounded by a soft pink light, glowing with warmth and open to the possibility of love.

Take the piece of parchment and the pink or red pen. Write down your intentions for this spell. If you are seeking to attract a new romantic relationship, be specific about the qualities you desire in a partner, such as kindness, understanding, or passion. If you are aiming to strengthen an existing relationship, focus on the aspects you wish to enhance, like communication, trust, or intimacy.

For example: "I attract a loving, harmonious relationship that is filled with joy, respect, and passion," or "May our love grow stronger, balanced, and full of understanding." As you write, infuse each word with your heartfelt desire for love that aligns with your highest good.

Fold the parchment and place it under the candle, allowing it to absorb the energy of the flame during the ritual.

3. Mixing the Love Herb Blend

In the small bowl or dish, combine the herbs: rose petals, jasmine, lavender, and basil. As you add each herb, focus on its specific properties and the qualities it brings to the relationship:

- **Rose:** *"Rose of love, passion, and fire, draw forth the love that I desire."*
- **Jasmine:** *"Jasmine sweet, bond of the soul, create a love that makes us whole."*
- **Lavender:** *"Lavender calm, soothing and true, bring balance and peace in all we do."*
- **Basil:** *"Basil of trust, fidelity's friend, let love and respect never end."*

Gently mix the herbs with your hands, visualizing them glowing with a soft, pink light. Feel the loving energy infusing the blend, ready to attract or enhance romantic love.

4. Charging the Crystals with Love Energy

One by one, hold each crystal in your hands and set its specific intention:

- **Rose Quartz:** Hold the rose quartz and say: *"Rose quartz, heart's embrace, fill my life with love's sweet grace. Open my heart, let love now flow, in passion and trust, may it grow."* Visualize a soft pink light emanating from the crystal, filling the room with warmth and love.
- **Green Aventurine:** Hold the green aventurine and say: *"Aventurine of balance, joy, and care, strengthen love, make it fair. Bring harmony and growth our way, let love and laughter guide our day."* Picture a green light radiating from the stone, creating an environment of stability and balance.

- **Amethyst:** Hold the amethyst and say: *"Amethyst of clarity and mind, open our hearts, our souls entwined. Enhance our bond, let truth be shown, in love's embrace, we are grown."* Visualize a soft purple light emanating from the crystal, promoting emotional clarity and understanding.

Place the charged crystals in the center of the herb blend, allowing their energies to merge and amplify the spell's intention.

5. Creating the Love Charm

Take the pink or red ribbon and tie it into a loose knot, saying:

"Ribbon of love, bind us tight, weave our hearts in joy and light. By this charm, our bond is sealed, in love's warm glow, our hearts revealed."

Sprinkle a pinch of the herb blend onto the ribbon, visualizing it absorbing the energies of love, harmony, and balance. Place the ribbon into the small pouch along with the crystals and the remaining herbs.

6. Sealing the Spell

Hold the pouch in front of the candle and focus on the flame. Imagine the light enveloping the pouch, sealing in the energies of love and harmony. Say the following incantation:

"By Venus's light and love's sweet grace, I seal this spell in time and space. Let love be true, let hearts align, in passion and trust, our spirits shine. So mote it be."

Visualize the flame growing brighter, sending out waves of love, warmth, and harmony into the universe. Trust that your intention for attracting or strengthening romantic love is being heard and set into motion.

7. Keeping the Love Charm

Place the pouch in a special place, such as under your pillow, in a drawer, or on an altar, to keep the spell's energy active. If you are in a relationship, consider sharing the charm with your partner as a symbol of your mutual commitment to nurturing and growing your love.

8. Reflecting on the Ritual

Sit quietly for a few moments and reflect on how you feel. Open your journal and write down your experience, including the intentions you set, the emotions that surfaced, and any insights you received during the ritual. In the days and weeks following, observe how love manifests in your life and how your relationship deepens or new opportunities for romance arise.

Tips for Maintaining Love and Harmony

- **Daily Affirmations:** Hold the rose quartz each morning and recite an affirmation like, "I am open to giving and receiving love in abundance," to keep the energy of love active.
- **Use the Herb Blend:** Sprinkle a small pinch of the herb blend in your room or near the bed to maintain an atmosphere of love and balance.
- **Refresh the Spell:** Perform this ritual periodically, especially during the waxing or full moon, to keep the energy of love vibrant and growing.

Final Thoughts

The "Balance of Hearts: Love Spell" is a tender and powerful ritual designed to attract new love or deepen the bond within an existing relationship. By focusing on balance, harmony, and mutual respect, this spell aligns with Libra's romantic ideals, ensuring that the love you cultivate is both passionate and stable. Using a blend of Libra's herbs and crystals, you call upon Venus's energy to open your heart, enhance connection, and create a relationship filled with joy, trust, and balance.

Love is not just about attraction but about nurturing a bond that grows stronger with time. As you work with this spell, let it remind you of the beauty and strength that come from love that is freely given, mutually shared, and lovingly maintained. By embracing the energy of balance and harmony, you create a love that flourishes, bringing warmth and light into every corner of your life.

Chapter 23: Scale of Fortune: Luck Spell

As a Libra, you have a natural affinity for balance, harmony, and the pursuit of good fortune. Ruled by Venus, the planet of beauty, love, and abundance, Libras are drawn to positive energies that bring joy, prosperity, and a sense of equilibrium. The "Scale of Fortune: Luck Spell" is crafted to help you invite good luck and fortune into your life by harnessing the energies of various crystals and symbols. This spell is designed to create a harmonious flow of positive energy, helping to align your life with opportunities and fortuitous circumstances.

Good luck is not just a random occurrence but can be influenced by setting intentions, creating positive vibrations, and inviting the universe's abundant energies into your life. Through the use of specific crystals and symbols, this spell aims to balance the scales in your favor, attracting luck, success, and prosperity. By performing this ritual, you open yourself to the natural ebb and flow of fortunate events, inviting them to become a regular part of your experience.

Crystals and Symbols for Luck and Fortune

Crystals have long been associated with attracting good luck, prosperity, and positive energy. Similarly, symbols such as the horseshoe, four-leaf clover, and lucky coin have been used in various cultures to draw in fortune. This spell combines these elements to create a powerful magnet for luck:

- **Crystals:**
    - **Citrine:** Known as the "Merchant's Stone," citrine attracts wealth, success, and abundance. It promotes a positive attitude and opens the mind to new possibilities.
    - **Green Aventurine:** The stone of luck, green aventurine enhances chances of success, encourages optimism, and attracts opportunities.
    - **Jade:** Symbolizes luck, prosperity, and protection, helping to attract good fortune and safeguard against negative energies.

- **Clear Quartz:** Amplifies intentions and the energies of other crystals, ensuring that your call for luck reaches the universe with strength and clarity.
- **Symbols:**
  - **Horseshoe:** Represents protection and good fortune. A horseshoe charm or symbol can be used to draw luck into your life.
  - **Four-Leaf Clover:** A classic symbol of luck, the four-leaf clover is said to bring good fortune and happiness.
  - **Lucky Coin:** A coin, particularly one that has sentimental or special meaning, symbolizes prosperity and the flow of wealth.

Materials Needed

- Citrine, green aventurine, jade, and clear quartz crystals
- A horseshoe charm, four-leaf clover, or lucky coin (or draw these symbols on paper if charms are unavailable)
- A gold or green candle (to symbolize wealth, luck, and success)
- A small bowl of sea salt (for purification)
- A piece of parchment or paper and a gold or green pen (to write intentions)
- A gold or green ribbon (to create a luck charm)
- A small pouch or cloth bag (to hold the charm)
- A lighter or matches
- A quiet, comfortable space for the ritual
- A journal or notebook (to record reflections)

Timing the Spell

This spell is best performed during a waxing moon, as the growing light of the moon supports the attraction of positive energy and new opportunities. For added potency, perform the ritual on a Thursday, ruled by Jupiter, the planet of luck, expansion, and fortune. The ideal time is in the morning or early afternoon, when the energy of the day is fresh and vibrant, symbolizing the incoming flow of good luck and fortune.

Steps for the Luck Spell

1. Preparing the Sacred Space

Select a quiet and comfortable area where you can perform the ritual undisturbed. Begin by cleansing the space with sea salt, sprinkling a few grains around to purify the environment and clear away any negative energy that might hinder the flow of luck. Place the gold or green candle in the center of your space, arranging the crystals, symbols, ribbon, pouch, parchment, and pen around it.

Light the candle, focusing on its warm, steady glow. Visualize its light expanding outward, creating a golden aura that invites good fortune and positivity into your life.

2. Setting Your Intentions for Luck

Close your eyes and take several deep breaths, inhaling the feeling of lightness and positivity. As you exhale, release any doubts, fears, or negative thoughts that might block the flow of luck. Visualize your entire being surrounded by a golden light, shining brightly and ready to attract the good fortune you seek.

Take the piece of parchment and the gold or green pen. Write down your intentions for the spell. Be specific about the kind of luck you wish to invite into your life, such as "I attract opportunities for success and prosperity," or "May fortune favor me in all my endeavors." As you write, infuse each word with a sense of joy, gratitude, and openness to receive.

When you have finished writing, fold the parchment and place it under the candle, allowing it to absorb the candle's energy throughout the ritual.

3. Activating the Crystals for Luck

One by one, hold each crystal in your hands and set its specific intention for attracting luck and fortune:

- **Citrine:** Hold the citrine and say: *"Citrine of gold, wealth's bright light, attract success, day and night. Open doors to luck and gain, bring joy and fortune, free from strain."* Visualize a golden light radiating from the crystal, filling the room with the energy of abundance and success.
- **Green Aventurine:** Hold the green aventurine and say: *"Aventurine of luck, jade's bright kin, bring opportunity, let luck begin. Draw fortune's favor, let it flow, in paths of green, let good things grow."* Picture a green light emanating from the stone, spreading out to create a magnetic field for luck.
- **Jade:** Hold the jade and say: *"Jade of fortune, stone of grace, guard my path, luck now embrace. Bring prosperity, wealth, and cheer, let fortune's blessings draw near."* Envision a soothing green energy surrounding you, providing both protection and attraction of good fortune.
- **Clear Quartz:** Hold the clear quartz and say: *"Quartz of clarity, pure and bright, amplify my call, send it to light. Luck and fortune, come to me, as I will it, so mote it be."* Imagine a white light emanating from the quartz, enhancing and amplifying the energies of the other crystals.

Place the crystals in a circle around the candle, allowing their energies to blend and amplify the spell's intention.

4. Choosing the Symbol of Fortune

Choose a symbol of fortune—a horseshoe charm, four-leaf clover, or lucky coin. If you do not have a physical charm, draw the symbol on a small piece of paper. Hold the symbol in your hands and say:

"Symbol of luck, charm of gold, bring fortune's light, let luck unfold. By this token, I now claim, good fortune's blessing, in my name."

Visualize the symbol glowing with a golden light, becoming a magnet for positive energy and luck.

5. Creating the Luck Charm

Cut a length of the gold or green ribbon and tie it into a loose knot, saying:

"Ribbon of fortune, tie so bright, weave my luck in golden light. By this charm, luck be near, bring joy and success, far and clear."

Sprinkle a pinch of sea salt onto the ribbon to purify it and the crystals to infuse it with the energies of luck. Place the ribbon, crystals, and symbol into the small pouch, sealing the charm with the power of the elements.

6. Sealing the Spell

Hold the pouch in front of the candle, focusing on the flame. Imagine the flame's light enveloping the pouch, sealing in the energies of luck, success, and fortune. Say the following incantation:

"By candle's flame and crystal's might, I seal this spell in golden light. Fortune's favor now comes to me, in luck and joy, as I will it be. So mote it be."

Visualize the candlelight shining brighter, sending waves of luck and positive energy into the universe. Trust that your intention for good fortune is being heard and will soon manifest in your life.

7. Keeping the Luck Charm

Place the pouch in a special location, such as in your bag, on your desk, or near an entryway, to keep the energy of the spell active. The charm will serve as a constant reminder and magnet for the luck and fortune you seek.

8. Reflecting on the Ritual

Sit quietly for a few moments, feeling the energies of luck and fortune surrounding you. Open your journal and write down your experience, including the intentions you set, the emotions that surfaced, and any insights you received during the ritual. In the days and weeks following, pay attention to how luck manifests in your life and how opportunities for success begin to present themselves.

Tips for Maintaining Good Luck

- **Daily Affirmations:** Hold the citrine crystal each morning and recite an affirmation like, "I am a magnet for good luck and fortune," to reinforce the spell's energy.
- **Use the Symbol:** Keep the symbol of fortune, such as the lucky coin or horseshoe charm, with you to maintain the flow of positive energy.
- **Refresh the Spell:** Perform this ritual periodically, especially during a waxing moon, to keep the energy of luck and fortune vibrant in your life.

Final Thoughts

The "Scale of Fortune: Luck Spell" is a powerful ritual designed to attract good luck, success, and prosperity. By combining the energies of various crystals and symbols, you align yourself with the natural flow of fortune, inviting opportunities and positive outcomes into your life. This spell resonates with Libra's desire for balance, harmony, and abundance, ensuring that the luck you attract not only brings joy but also creates a sense of stability and well-being.

Luck is not merely about chance; it is about being open to the universe's gifts and positioning yourself to receive them. As you work with this spell, let it remind you of the power of intention and the harmony that comes from aligning your energy with the flow of fortune. By embracing the scale of fortune, you invite the universe to tip the balance in your favor, filling your life with joy, success, and endless possibilities.

Chapter 24: Crystal Clear: Clarity and Focus Spell

Mental clarity and focus are essential for maintaining the balance and harmony that Libras crave in their daily lives. As an air sign, Libra is naturally inclined toward deep thinking and analysis. However, the constant weighing of options and consideration of different perspectives can sometimes lead to mental clutter, indecision, and a lack of focus. The "Crystal Clear: Clarity and Focus Spell" is designed to help clear mental fog, sharpen focus, and bring a sense of direction using the powerful properties of clear quartz and the soothing energy of moonlight.

Clear quartz, known as the "Master Healer" in crystal work, is renowned for its ability to amplify intentions, dispel negativity, and promote mental clarity. When combined with the calming and purifying influence of moonlight, this spell creates a sacred space for mental rejuvenation and focus. This ritual is ideal for situations where you need to make important decisions, gain perspective, or simply clear your mind for more effective concentration.

The Power of Clear Quartz and Moonlight

- **Clear Quartz:** Clear quartz is a versatile and powerful crystal that can be programmed with any intention, making it perfect for spells related to clarity and focus. It enhances mental clarity, aids in concentration, and clears away confusion or negative thoughts. Its amplifying properties also help to magnify the energy of your intentions, ensuring they are directed with strength and precision.

- **Moonlight:** Moonlight has been revered in magical practices for its cleansing, calming, and nurturing qualities. Bathing in moonlight, particularly during the full or waxing phases, helps to purify the mind, release mental clutter, and promote inner peace. By incorporating moonlight into this spell, you draw upon its tranquil energy to wash away distractions and bring a sense of clarity.

Materials Needed

- A clear quartz crystal (preferably a point or cluster for focus and direction)
- A white or light blue candle (to symbolize purity and mental clarity)
- A small bowl of water (for cleansing the crystal)
- A piece of parchment or paper and a blue pen (to write intentions)
- A silver or white cloth (to create a moonlit altar space)
- A quiet, comfortable space with access to moonlight (preferably outside or near a window)
- A journal or notebook (to record reflections)
- A lighter or matches

Timing the Spell

The ideal time to perform this spell is during the waxing moon or on the night of the full moon, when the moon's energy is at its peak for cleansing and illumination. The moonlight's purifying properties will help wash away mental fog and distractions, while its nurturing energy promotes focus and calmness. Conduct the ritual at night, preferably when the moon is high and visible, to fully harness its light and energy.

Steps for the Clarity and Focus Spell

1. Preparing the Sacred Space

Choose a quiet, comfortable area where you can perform the ritual, preferably with access to moonlight. Spread the silver or white cloth on a flat surface to create an altar space that reflects the moon's energy. Arrange the clear quartz crystal, candle, bowl of water, parchment, and pen on the cloth.

Begin by lighting the candle, focusing on its steady flame as a beacon of mental clarity and purity. Let its light create a serene atmosphere, invoking a sense of calm and focus.

2. Cleansing the Clear Quartz with Water

Hold the clear quartz crystal in your hands and take a moment to connect with its energy. Close your eyes and breathe deeply, feeling the crystal's cool, calming vibration in your palms. As you exhale, release any mental tension or fog, allowing your mind to begin clearing.

Gently dip the crystal into the bowl of water, saying:

"Water pure, crystal clear, cleanse this stone, remove all fear. Let its light now amplify, focus my mind, clear my eye."

Visualize the water washing away any lingering energies from the crystal, leaving it pure and ready to receive your intentions for mental clarity and focus.

3. Setting Your Intentions for Clarity and Focus

Take the piece of parchment and the blue pen. Write down your intentions for this spell, focusing on what you wish to gain in terms of mental clarity and focus. Be specific about the areas of your life where you seek direction, whether it's making a decision, completing a project, or simply finding peace of mind.

Examples of intentions could be: "I seek clarity of thought and focus in my daily tasks," or "May my mind be clear and free of distractions, allowing me to see my path forward." As you write, imagine your mind becoming like the clear quartz itself—pure, focused, and filled with light.

Fold the parchment and place it on the altar, allowing it to absorb the energy of the candlelight and moonlight.

4. Charging the Crystal with Moonlight

Hold the clear quartz crystal up to the moonlight, whether you are outside or near a window. Visualize the moonlight streaming down into the crystal, filling it with a cool, luminous energy. Feel the light washing over you, calming your mind and enhancing your mental clarity.

Say the following incantation:

"Moonlight pure, shining bright, fill this crystal with your light. Clear my mind, sharpen my sight, focus my thoughts, guide me right."

Visualize the crystal glowing with the moon's energy, becoming a beacon of clarity and focus. Imagine its light penetrating your mind, clearing away any fog, distractions, or confusion.

5. Meditating with the Crystal

Sit comfortably and hold the charged clear quartz in both hands. Close your eyes and take several deep, slow breaths. As you inhale, imagine the crystal's light filling your entire body with calmness and focus. As you exhale, release any remaining tension or mental clutter.

Allow yourself to sink into a meditative state. Picture your thoughts organizing themselves, like stars in the night sky, each one becoming clear, precise, and luminous. Feel a sense of mental spaciousness and tranquility, as if your mind has been bathed in the pure light of the moon.

Stay in this meditative state for several minutes, focusing on the sensation of clarity and focus radiating from the crystal. Trust that this energy is clearing your mind and sharpening your mental faculties.

6. Sealing the Spell

When you feel ready, gently place the crystal on the parchment. Let it rest there as you blow out the candle, allowing the smoke to carry your intentions into the universe. As you extinguish the flame, say:

"By crystal's light and moon's embrace, I seal this spell in time and space. Clarity flows, focus stays, guide my mind through all my days. So mote it be."

Visualize the moonlight and the crystal's energy merging, sealing the spell and embedding its effects within you.

7. Keeping the Crystal Nearby

Place the charged clear quartz crystal somewhere accessible, such as on your desk, by your bed, or in your bag. The crystal will serve as a touchstone for mental clarity and focus whenever you need it. You can also carry it with you during important tasks, meetings, or study sessions to maintain a clear, focused mindset.

8. Reflecting on the Ritual

Sit quietly for a few moments and notice how your mind feels. Open your journal and write down your experience, including the intentions you set, the emotions that surfaced, and any sensations you felt during the ritual. In the days following, pay attention to how your mental clarity and focus improve, and note any insights or decisions that become easier to make.

Tips for Maintaining Mental Clarity and Focus

- **Daily Use:** Each morning, hold the clear quartz crystal in your hand and repeat a simple affirmation, such as "My mind is clear, and my focus is strong," to reinforce the spell's energy.
- **Moonlight Recharge:** Place the crystal in moonlight regularly, especially during the full moon, to cleanse and recharge its energy.
- **Meditative Breaks:** When feeling mentally scattered, take a short break to hold the crystal, close your eyes, and breathe deeply, reconnecting with its clarity-enhancing energy.

Final Thoughts

The "Crystal Clear: Clarity and Focus Spell" is a gentle yet powerful way to cleanse the mind and enhance mental focus. By combining the properties of clear quartz with the soothing energy of moonlight, you create a sacred space for mental rejuvenation, helping you to approach tasks, decisions, and daily life with a sense of direction and ease. This spell aligns with Libra's natural affinity for balance and clear thinking, providing a tool for navigating life's complexities with grace and precision.

Mental clarity is not just about making decisions but about creating an inner space where thoughts can flow freely, undisturbed by distractions or doubts. As you work with this spell, let it remind you of the beauty that comes from a clear, focused mind, allowing you to embrace your Libran qualities of thoughtful consideration and balanced perspective in all aspects of life.

Chapter 25: Lunar Balance: Moon Phase Rituals

The moon has a profound influence on our emotions, actions, and overall energy. As a Libra, you are naturally sensitive to the ebbs and flows of the lunar cycle, making moon phase rituals an ideal way to harmonize your emotions and align your actions. The moon's phases represent different aspects of the life cycle—from beginnings to growth, release, and reflection. By working with these phases, you can enhance your balance and take intentional steps toward your goals, personal growth, and emotional well-being.

In this chapter, we explore the significance of each moon phase and how to use its energy to align your emotions and actions. Each phase presents a unique opportunity to focus on different aspects of your life, from manifesting desires during the New Moon to releasing negativity during the Waning Moon. These rituals help you work in harmony with the moon's natural rhythm, ensuring that your efforts are both empowered and aligned with the universe's energy.

The Moon Phases and Their Energies

The moon cycle consists of eight phases, each offering its own vibrational frequency and influence over our lives. By understanding these phases and performing specific rituals aligned with them, you can harness the moon's power to achieve emotional balance, spiritual growth, and goal fulfillment.

1. **New Moon:** The time of new beginnings, planting seeds of intention, and setting goals.
2. **Waxing Crescent:** A phase for nurturing intentions, building momentum, and attracting positive energy.
3. **First Quarter:** A period for taking action, overcoming obstacles, and making decisions.
4. **Waxing Gibbous:** A time to refine your intentions, reassess your goals, and boost motivation.

5. **Full Moon:** The peak of energy, ideal for manifestation, celebrating achievements, and releasing what no longer serves you.
6. **Waning Gibbous:** A phase for expressing gratitude, sharing wisdom, and preparing for release.
7. **Last Quarter:** A time for letting go, breaking habits, and clearing obstacles.
8. **Waning Crescent:** A phase of rest, reflection, and introspection before the new cycle begins.

Moon Phase Rituals for Harmonizing Emotions and Actions

Each phase's ritual is designed to help you harness the specific energy of the moon at that time, focusing on emotional balance and aligned action.

1. New Moon Ritual: Setting Intentions and Planting Seeds

The New Moon represents a fresh start, a blank slate. It's the perfect time to set your intentions for the lunar cycle ahead. In this ritual, you will plant the seeds of what you wish to grow, focusing on the energies of new beginnings and potential.

Materials Needed:

- A black or white candle (to represent the new beginning and a clean slate)
- A small pot of soil and seeds (or a plant to symbolize growth)
- A piece of parchment and a pen

Ritual Steps:

1. Light the candle to symbolize the new energy of the moon.
2. Hold the seeds in your hand and close your eyes. Visualize the new opportunities and goals you wish to plant during this cycle. Feel the excitement and potential they hold.
3. Write down your intentions on the parchment, focusing on what you wish to manifest. Be specific and positive in your wording.

4. Plant the seeds in the pot of soil, saying: *"New Moon's light, dark and clear, I plant these seeds, my goals draw near. As these seeds grow, so do I, with lunar strength, I reach the sky."*

5. Keep the pot in a place where you can tend to it, using it as a reminder of your intentions as they develop.

Focus: Manifesting new intentions and projects with a sense of excitement and hope.

2. Waxing Crescent Ritual: Building Energy and Nurturing Intentions

The **Waxing Crescent** phase is a time of growth and building energy. This is when you nurture your intentions and begin attracting the positive energies needed to manifest them.

Materials Needed:

- A green candle (for growth and abundance)
- A small bowl of water
- A piece of green aventurine or citrine

Ritual Steps:

1. Light the green candle, focusing on the energy of growth and abundance.

2. Hold the crystal in your hand and dip your fingers in the bowl of water. Sprinkle the water around your space, saying: *"Crescent moon, wax and grow, nurture my dreams, let them show. With every step, with every day, I build my path, I find my way."*

3. Place the crystal in a place where you can see it daily, reminding you to take steps toward nurturing your intentions.

Focus: Attracting the energy and resources needed to bring your intentions to life.

3. First Quarter Ritual: Taking Action and Overcoming Obstacles

The First Quarter moon marks a time for action and decision-making. It is a period of challenge, requiring you to face obstacles head-on and push forward toward your goals.

Materials Needed:

- A red or orange candle (for courage and motivation)
- A piece of clear quartz
- A piece of parchment and a pen

Ritual Steps:

1. Light the candle, focusing on the flame as a symbol of courage and determination.
2. Write down the challenges or obstacles you are facing in relation to your goals. Next to each one, write an action you can take to overcome it.
3. Hold the clear quartz in your hand and say: *"Quarter moon, half in light, give me strength, guide my sight. With clear intent and courage bright, I face my fears, I win the fight."*
4. Place the quartz on the list, sealing your commitment to take action.

Focus: Taking decisive actions to move forward and overcoming challenges with courage.

4. Waxing Gibbous Ritual: Refining and Adjusting Intentions

The Waxing Gibbous moon is the phase to reassess, refine, and adjust your intentions. It is a time to revisit your goals, make adjustments, and boost motivation.

Materials Needed:

- A purple or yellow candle (for wisdom and insight)
- Lavender or rosemary essential oil
- A piece of parchment and a pen

Ritual Steps:

1. Light the candle and anoint your forehead and wrists with the essential oil.
2. Sit quietly and reflect on the progress you've made so far. Write down any changes you wish to make to your plans or new insights that have come to you.
3. Say aloud: *"Gibbous moon, almost bright, help me see, clear my sight. Refine my path, adjust my aim, with focus true, I play the game."*
4. Fold the parchment and place it near the candle until it burns out, symbolizing the refinement of your intentions.

Focus: Adjusting and refining your plans, preparing for the final push toward manifestation.

5. Full Moon Ritual: Manifestation and Release

The Full Moon is the climax of the lunar cycle, representing completion, manifestation, and celebration. It is also an excellent time to release anything that no longer serves you.

Materials Needed:

- A silver or white candle (for illumination and purity)
- A bowl of water
- A piece of rose quartz

Ritual Steps:

1. Light the candle and place the bowl of water under the moonlight (or near a window where moonlight is visible).
2. Hold the rose quartz and focus on the intentions you set during the New Moon. Visualize them manifesting and filling your life with joy and fulfillment.
3. Dip your fingers into the water and sprinkle it around you, saying: *"Full moon bright, at your peak, bring forth my dreams, the things I seek. With open heart, I now release, what holds me back, bring me peace."*
4. Visualize any negative thoughts or obstacles being washed away with the moonlight.

Focus: Manifesting your desires and releasing negativity.

6. Waning Gibbous Ritual: Gratitude and Sharing

The Waning Gibbous phase is a time for gratitude and sharing the wisdom you've gained. Reflect on what you've achieved and express thanks for the progress.

Materials Needed:

- A pink candle (for gratitude and love)
- A piece of parchment and a pen

Ritual Steps:

1. Light the pink candle and sit quietly in its glow.
2. Write down what you are grateful for, focusing on the progress, insights, and manifestations you've experienced during the cycle.
3. Say: *"Gibbous moon, waning light, I give thanks, in your sight. With open heart and grateful cheer, I share my joy, I hold it dear."*

Focus: Gratitude and sharing the fruits of your intentions.

7. Last Quarter Ritual: Releasing and Letting Go

The Last Quarter moon is a time for letting go, breaking habits, and clearing out what no longer serves you. This phase encourages reflection and release.

Materials Needed:

- A black candle (for release and transformation)
- A piece of parchment and a pen
- A fireproof dish

Ritual Steps:

1. Light the candle, focusing on its flame as a symbol of transformation.
2. Write down anything you wish to release, such as negative habits, thoughts, or situations.
3. Hold the paper over the flame (carefully) and drop it into the fireproof dish to burn, saying: *"Quarter moon, dark and clear, take away what I hold near. I release, I let it go, cleanse my spirit, let it flow."*

Focus: Releasing negativity, clearing space for new growth.

8. Waning Crescent Ritual: Rest and Reflect

The Waning Crescent phase is a time for rest, reflection, and intro-spection. It is a period of stillness before the next cycle begins.

Materials Needed:

- A blue or white candle (for peace and reflection)
- A journal or notebook

Ritual Steps:

1. Light the candle and sit comfortably.
2. Spend time reflecting on the entire lunar cycle. Write in your jour-nal about what you have learned, experienced, and released.
3. Say: *"Crescent moon, waning slow, bring me peace, let wisdom grow. As I rest, as I dream, cleanse my soul in moon's soft gleam."*

Focus: Resting, reflecting on your journey, and preparing for a new cycle.

Final Thoughts

The "Lunar Balance: Moon Phase Rituals" chapter provides you with an array of spells designed to align your emotions and actions with the natural ebb and flow of the moon's energies. By following these ritu-als, you create a practice that honors the moon's cycles, helping you stay in balance, manifest your desires, and release what no longer serves you. As a Libra, working with the moon allows you to embrace your innate desire for harmony, ensuring that your actions are in tune with the uni-verse's rhythms.

The moon's phases remind us that life is a cycle of growth, change, and renewal. By aligning with these cycles, you not only harness the moon's powerful energy but also cultivate a deeper understanding of your own emotional and spiritual journey. Let these rituals guide you in creating a life of balance, harmony, and intentional action.

Chapter 26: The Libran Knot: Binding Spell

Libras are naturally inclined toward harmony, justice, and fairness in their interactions and pursuits. However, there are times when protecting your interests, values, and personal energy becomes necessary to maintain balance in your life. The "Libran Knot: Binding Spell" is a protective ritual designed to safeguard your well-being, guard against negative influences, and secure your intentions. This spell uses the symbolic power of knots and ribbons, along with focused intention, to bind what could potentially disrupt your equilibrium, ensuring that your interests remain protected.

Binding spells are not inherently harmful; rather, they are powerful protective tools used to set boundaries and shield against negativity or unwanted influences. By focusing on your intention, this spell creates a barrier that locks away what could disturb your peace and stability. The knotting of the ribbon represents the act of securing your space, energy, and interests in a way that is both respectful and firm. With Libra's affinity for balance, this spell is performed not out of malice but as a means of self-care, ensuring that you maintain control over your own life and emotions.

The Symbolic Power of Knots and Ribbons

- **Knots:** Throughout history, knots have been used in magical practices to bind, secure, and control energy. In this spell, knotting the ribbon symbolizes your act of securing your intentions and protecting your interests, locking them away from negativity and outside interference.

- **Ribbon:** The ribbon represents the flow of your intentions and energy. By choosing a color that aligns with your purpose (such as white for purity, blue for calm, or black for protection), you harness its vibrational qualities to strengthen the binding.

Materials Needed

- A length of ribbon (approximately 18–24 inches) in a color that represents your intention:
    ◦ **White:** For purity, peace, and general protection.
    ◦ **Black:** For strong protection, warding off negative energy.
    ◦ **Blue:** For calming and emotional protection.
    ◦ **Pink:** For self-love and nurturing.
- A small piece of parchment or paper and a pen
- A black or white candle (to represent protection and binding)
- A small bowl of sea salt (for cleansing the space)
- A quiet, comfortable space to perform the ritual
- A lighter or matches
- A pouch or cloth bag (to keep the bound knot safe)
- A journal or notebook (to record reflections)

Timing the Spell

The ideal time to perform this spell is during the waning moon, particularly during the Last Quarter or Waning Crescent phases, when the moon's energy supports the release, banishment, and protection against unwanted influences. If you wish to align the spell with the planetary energies of Libra, you can also perform it on a Friday, the day ruled by Venus, which promotes balance and self-care.

Steps for the Binding Spell

1. Preparing the Sacred Space

Begin by selecting a quiet, comfortable area where you will not be disturbed. Cleanse the space by sprinkling sea salt around you, creating a protective circle that helps to purify and seal the environment. Place the ribbon, candle, parchment, pen, and pouch on a flat surface in front of you.

Light the black or white candle, focusing on its flame as a source of strength and protection. As the candle burns, envision its light forming a shield around you, creating a safe space for the spell.

2. Setting Your Intentions for Protection

Close your eyes and take several deep breaths, inhaling calmness and exhaling any stress or anxiety. Visualize the situation, person, or energy that you wish to protect yourself against. It could be a negative influence, an unhealthy habit, or anything that threatens your peace and balance.

Take the piece of parchment and pen, and write down your intention for the binding. Be clear and specific, focusing on what you wish to bind and why. For example: "I bind negative influences from affecting my well-being," or "I secure my intentions and protect my energy from harm." Ensure that your wording is respectful and mindful, as the purpose of this spell is self-protection, not harm.

Fold the parchment and place it near the candle to absorb its protective energy.

3. Empowering the Ribbon with Intention

Hold the ribbon in your hands, closing your eyes to connect with its energy. Visualize the ribbon glowing with the color you have chosen, vibrating with the intention you have set. Imagine the ribbon becoming a conduit for your will, ready to bind and protect what is sacred to you.

Say aloud:

"Ribbon bright, strong and true, I bind what harms, what breaks in two. With knots of strength, I now create, a shield of peace, a guarded state."

Feel the power of your intention flowing into the ribbon, filling it with protective energy.

4. Knotting the Binding Spell

Now, begin knotting the ribbon. You will tie three knots in total, each one representing a layer of protection and the binding of negative energy. As you tie each knot, repeat the following incantation:

- **First Knot:** While tying the first knot, say: *"By the first knot, I do bind, protection around, peace in mind."*
- **Second Knot:** As you tie the second knot, say: *"By the second knot, harm stays away, I secure my space, night and day."*
- **Third Knot:** For the final knot, say: *"By the third knot, strength I seal, my interests bound, my peace is real."*

As you tie each knot, visualize the energy of the binding becoming stronger, forming an impenetrable barrier around your intentions and your energy. Imagine the knots tightening around the unwanted influence, securing it in place and keeping it from disturbing your life.

5. Sealing the Binding

Hold the knotted ribbon over the flame of the candle (being careful not to burn it) to seal the energy. Say:

"Candle's flame, burn so bright, seal this binding, in peace and light. By knot and will, I now decree, what I bind shall stay, so mote it be."

Visualize the light of the candle enveloping the ribbon, sealing your intention and the binding you have created. Feel the energy solidify, knowing that what you have bound is now secured and cannot cross the protective boundary you have established.

6. Storing the Knot

Place the knotted ribbon and the folded parchment into the pouch or cloth bag. Keep this pouch in a safe place, such as a drawer, on your altar, or under your pillow. This pouch serves as a symbol of your binding spell, holding the energy of your protection and intentions. If you ever feel the need to release the binding, you can simply untie the knots in a future ritual to dissolve the spell's effects.

7. Reflecting on the Ritual

Sit quietly for a few moments and reflect on the experience. Open your journal and write down your thoughts, the intentions you set, and any sensations or emotions you felt during the ritual. In the days following, observe how the energy in your environment changes and how the protection you have set up affects your peace of mind.

Tips for Reinforcing the Binding

- **Regular Cleansing:** Periodically cleanse the knotted ribbon by placing the pouch in moonlight or near a candle's flame (without burning it) to keep its protective energy active.
- **Daily Affirmations:** Hold the pouch each morning and recite a simple affirmation, such as "I am safe, my peace is guarded," to re-inforce the spell's protection.
- **Meditative Focus:** If you feel the binding weakening, take a moment to visualize the knots tightening and the protective barrier growing stronger around you.

Final Thoughts

The "Libran Knot: Binding Spell" is a powerful way to protect your interests and energy, ensuring that you maintain balance and harmony in your life. This spell is not about harming others but about securing your well-being and creating boundaries that protect you from un-wanted influences. As a Libra, you value peace, fairness, and emotional equilibrium, and this binding spell is a reflection of your commitment to preserving these qualities in your life.

Binding spells, when performed with respect and clarity of inten-tion, can serve as effective tools for self-care and protection. Remember that this ritual is not an act of aggression but an affirmation of your right to create a life free from negativity and harm. By knotting the ribbon and focusing on your intention, you lock away what could disrupt your peace, creating a shield that upholds your balance and serenity.

Let this spell be a reminder of the strength and wisdom you possess as a Libra. When you take steps to protect your energy and interests, you honor the balance that you seek in all things, creating a space where you can flourish and thrive.

Chapter 27: Wind of Change: Letting Go Spell

As an air sign, Libras are closely connected to the element of wind, which symbolizes freedom, change, and the power of the mind. However, like the gentle breeze that can turn into a storm, your emotions and thoughts can sometimes become turbulent, filled with lingering negative energies and burdens from the past. When these negative influences build up, they can disrupt your natural state of harmony and balance. The "Wind of Change: Letting Go Spell" harnesses the power of the wind to help you release these burdens, allowing you to move forward with a renewed sense of lightness and freedom.

The element of wind is associated with mental clarity, transformation, and the movement of energy. It carries away what no longer serves us and opens space for new beginnings. By using wind-themed elements, such as feathers, incense smoke, and breath, this spell creates a channel for releasing negativity and past burdens, restoring your emotional balance. This ritual aligns perfectly with Libra's need for harmony and peace, offering a cathartic way to cleanse your spirit and embrace change.

The Symbolism of Wind in Letting Go Rituals

Wind is one of the most powerful elements in spellcraft due to its fluidity and ability to change direction. It can be both gentle and forceful, carrying your intentions far and wide. In this spell, the wind acts as a transformative force, sweeping away the negative energies that weigh you down. By invoking the wind, you align with its freeing qualities, allowing yourself to let go of what is no longer beneficial.

- **Feather:** Represents the lightness and freedom of the wind, helping to release emotional burdens.
- **Incense Smoke:** Symbolizes the unseen currents of energy, purifying your space and carrying away negativity.

- **Breath:** Acts as a conduit for wind, guiding your intentions outward as you exhale.

Materials Needed

- A feather (preferably white or gray to symbolize purity and release)
- Incense (sandalwood, sage, or lavender for purification)
- A small bowl of saltwater (for cleansing)
- A piece of parchment or paper and a black or blue pen
- A blue or white candle (to represent the wind and emotional clarity)
- A quiet, outdoor space (if possible) where you can feel the natural breeze
- A lighter or matches
- A journal or notebook (to record reflections)

Timing the Spell

This spell is best performed during a waning moon, especially during the Waning Gibbous or Last Quarter phases, which support release, letting go, and transformation. If possible, perform the ritual on a windy day to further connect with the natural element of air. Morning or early afternoon is ideal, as these times represent the beginning of a new day and the opportunity for change.

Steps for the Letting Go Spell

1. Preparing the Sacred Space

Choose a quiet outdoor space where you can feel the natural breeze. If this is not possible, find a space indoors near an open window to let the wind flow into the room. Begin by placing the candle, feather, incense, bowl of saltwater, parchment, and pen in front of you.

Light the blue or white candle to invoke the presence of the wind and the air element. Let its flame represent clarity and the power of change. If outside, take a moment to breathe in the fresh air, feeling its coolness as it flows around you.

2. Cleansing and Setting Intentions

Dip your fingers into the bowl of saltwater and sprinkle a few drops around your space to purify it. This will cleanse the area of any lingering negativity and prepare it for the release process.

Close your eyes and take several deep breaths, inhaling the fresh air and exhaling any tension or heaviness you may be carrying. Visualize the air around you filling with light, becoming a supportive force for transformation. Focus on the negative energies, emotions, or past burdens that you wish to let go of. Identify what is holding you back, such as fears, regrets, or unhealthy attachments.

Take the parchment and pen, and write down everything you want to release. Be specific and honest, allowing your emotions to flow freely onto the paper. This could include phrases like, "I release my fear of failure," or "I let go of past regrets that weigh me down." Writing these down serves as a symbolic act of acknowledging what you are ready to release.

3. Invoking the Wind's Power with the Feather

Pick up the feather and hold it in both hands. Close your eyes and take a deep breath, imagining the feather filling with the power of the wind. Visualize a breeze gathering around you, swirling with energy that is both calming and transformative. Feel the wind's gentle touch, ready to carry away your burdens.

Say aloud:

"Wind of change, strong and free, take these burdens, carry them from me. Feather light, lift my pain, clear my mind, let peace remain."

As you speak, imagine the feather absorbing your intentions for release, becoming a vessel for the energy you wish to let go of.

4. Burning the Incense for Purification

Light the incense, holding it in your hand as it begins to smoke. The rising smoke symbolizes the movement of energy, purifying your space and intentions. Wave the feather gently through the smoke, visualizing the negativity being lifted and carried away by the wind. The smoke represents the currents of the air element, ready to disperse the burdens you have written down.

Say:

"Incense smoke, rise and flow, cleanse my spirit, let go, let go. As wind takes flight, so shall these fears, leave behind the weight of years."

As you speak, feel a sense of lightness beginning to take hold, as though the burdens are being lifted from your shoulders and transformed into the wind's energy.

5. Releasing the Written Intentions

Take the parchment where you have written your burdens. If you are outside, hold it up to the wind, allowing the breeze to pass over it, symbolizing the release of these burdens into the air. If inside, hold it near the open window, visualizing the wind taking your intentions and carrying them far away.

Tear the parchment into small pieces, letting each piece fall to the ground or into a bowl as you say:

"With each tear, I break the chain, release the hurt, dissolve the pain. Wind, take these words, far from here, bring me peace, bring me clear."

Feel the sense of release with each tear, allowing your mind and heart to become lighter.

6. Sealing the Spell with Breath

To complete the spell, close your eyes and take a deep breath in. Hold it for a moment, gathering any remaining tension or negativity within you. Then, exhale forcefully, blowing the air out as though you are expelling the burdens from your body. Repeat this three times, each exhale representing the final release of what you are letting go.

As you take the last breath, say:

"Wind of change, now set me free, clear my mind, let peace be. I release, I let it go, by breath and air, new life shall flow."

Imagine the wind around you swirling, sweeping away the last remnants of your burdens, leaving you feeling light, clear, and renewed.

7. Closing the Ritual

Gently blow out the candle, watching the smoke rise and dissipate into the air. Visualize the candle's flame sealing your intentions for release and the wind carrying away what you no longer need.

Place the feather on your altar or a special place in your home as a reminder of the power of release and change. The feather will serve as a talisman, symbolizing your newfound freedom and the lightness of being that comes with letting go.

8. Reflecting on the Ritual

Sit quietly for a few moments, noticing how you feel. Open your journal and write down your experience, including what you released, how the ritual made you feel, and any insights or emotions that surfaced. In the days following, observe how your emotional state changes and how the act of letting go creates new space for positive energy in your life.

Tips for Maintaining Emotional Clarity

- **Regular Wind Rituals:** Incorporate the wind element into your regular spiritual practice by taking deep breaths outside or waving a feather when you feel overwhelmed, helping you reconnect with its freeing energy.
- **Daily Affirmations:** Use affirmations like "I release what no longer serves me" each morning to keep your intentions of letting go active.
- **Wind Meditation:** When feeling burdened, sit in a windy place, close your eyes, and visualize the wind sweeping away any lingering negative thoughts or emotions.

Final Thoughts

The "Wind of Change: Letting Go Spell" offers a powerful and gentle way to release negativity, past burdens, and stagnant energy from your life. By harnessing the transformative power of the wind, you align with Libra's natural affinity for balance and harmony, creating a space for renewal and positive change. This ritual encourages you to let go with grace, embracing the freedom and clarity that comes with releasing what no longer serves you.

Letting go is not an act of weakness, but a testament to your strength and commitment to maintaining peace and balance in your life. As you work with this spell, allow the wind's energy to remind you that change is a natural part of growth. By freeing yourself from the past, you open the way for new opportunities, joy, and a lightness of being that is truly liberating.

Chapter 28: Scales of Creation: Manifestation Spell

Manifestation is the art of bringing desires into reality by aligning thoughts, emotions, and actions with the universe's energy. As a Libra, ruled by Venus, you naturally possess an affinity for balance, beauty, and harmony. The "Scales of Creation: Manifestation Spell" harnesses this innate Libran ability by using a combination of balanced elements in your environment to create a powerful manifestation ritual. This spell focuses on drawing in the energy of the four elements—earth, air, fire, and water—to bring your desires into alignment with the universe, promoting their realization.

The key to manifestation lies in balance. When you achieve harmony between your intentions and the elements around you, you create a space where the energy can flow freely toward your desires. This spell uses symbols and tools from each element, ensuring that the energies are balanced, which is especially suited for Libra's need for equilibrium. By incorporating earth's stability, air's movement, fire's passion, and water's fluidity, you channel a potent force that helps bring your goals and dreams into reality.

The Role of the Elements in Manifestation

- **Earth:** Represents stability, grounding, and the physical realm. In this spell, earth anchors your desires and gives them a solid foundation for growth.
- **Air:** Symbolizes intellect, clarity, and communication. Air helps you articulate your intentions clearly and sends them out into the universe.
- **Fire:** Represents passion, transformation, and action. Fire energizes your desires and gives them the power to manifest.
- **Water:** Symbolizes emotion, intuition, and flow. Water adds a nurturing energy, allowing your desires to grow and adapt.

Materials Needed

- A small bowl of soil or a potted plant (to represent earth)
- Incense or a feather (to represent air)
- A red or orange candle (to represent fire)
- A bowl of water (to represent water)
- A piece of parchment or paper and a green or gold pen (to write intentions)
- A small crystal (clear quartz, rose quartz, or citrine) to amplify your intentions
- A quiet, comfortable space where you can arrange the elements
- A lighter or matches
- A journal or notebook (to record reflections)

Timing the Spell

This manifestation spell is best performed during a waxing or full moon, as these phases are associated with growth, abundance, and the amplification of intentions. For added potency, perform the ritual on a Friday, which is ruled by Venus, the planet of love, beauty, and attraction. Choose a time when you feel relaxed, focused, and free from distractions—early evening is ideal, as it represents the transition between day and night, symbolizing the bridging of your desires from thought into reality.

Steps for the Manifestation Spell

1. Preparing the Sacred Space

Find a quiet, comfortable area where you can arrange the elements in a circle around you. If possible, choose a space where you can sit cross-legged within this circle to feel fully immersed in the balanced energy. Begin by placing the four elements—earth (bowl of soil or plant), air (incense or feather), fire (candle), and water (bowl)—in a circle around you.

As you arrange these elements, visualize them creating a balanced and harmonious space. Feel the energy of each element interacting and blending with the others, creating a powerful force that surrounds and supports you.

2. Grounding with Earth

Start by connecting with the element of earth, which provides the foundation for manifestation. Take the bowl of soil or the potted plant in your hands. Close your eyes and take several deep breaths, feeling the grounding energy of the earth beneath you. Visualize your desires taking root in the soil, just as a seed would.

Say aloud:

"Earth, strong and steady, ground my desires, make them ready. With roots deep and soil firm, let my dreams grow, let them affirm."

Place the bowl of soil or plant in front of you to represent the foundation of your manifestation.

3. Sending Intentions with Air

Next, focus on the element of air, which helps carry your intentions to the universe. If using incense, light it now, allowing the smoke to drift and swirl around you. If using a feather, hold it gently in your hand and wave it slowly through the air.

Take the parchment and pen, and write down your intentions clearly and specifically. Be as detailed as possible, focusing on what you wish to manifest in your life. It could be a new job, love, financial abundance, or a personal goal. For example, "I attract a fulfilling career that brings me joy and prosperity," or "I welcome love that is kind, balanced, and nurturing."

As you write, feel the element of air surrounding you, helping to articulate your desires with clarity.

Say aloud:

"Air, light and free, carry my words, bring them to be. With breath of life, intentions fly, reach the stars, touch the sky."

Place the parchment near the incense or feather, allowing the element of air to lift your words into the universe.

4. Energizing with Fire

Now, turn your focus to the element of fire, which provides the passion and energy needed to bring your desires to life. Light the candle, focusing on its flame as a symbol of your inner drive and the transformative power of fire.

Hold the crystal in your hands and gaze into the flame. Visualize the flame growing larger, consuming any doubts or obstacles that may hinder your manifestation. See the flame energizing your intentions, giving them the power to manifest.

Say:

"Fire bright, passion's spark, light the way, guide my heart. With flame's power, bring to me, the dreams I seek, the goals I see."

Place the crystal next to the candle to absorb its fiery energy.

5. Nurturing with Water

Finally, connect with the element of water, which nurtures your intentions and allows them to flow into reality. Take the bowl of water and hold it in your hands. Close your eyes and visualize your desires flowing like water, adapting and growing in harmony with your life.

Say:

"Water clear, fluid and free, nurture my dreams, let them be. With gentle flow, with calming grace, bring to my life, blessings in place."

Dip your fingers into the water and sprinkle a few drops around you, creating a nurturing circle that encourages the growth of your manifestation.

6. Sealing the Spell with the Elements

Now that all the elements have been invoked and balanced, it's time to seal the spell. Place your hands over the parchment where you have written your intentions. Close your eyes and visualize each element coming together—earth providing a stable foundation, air lifting your desires to the universe, fire energizing and transforming, and water nurturing the manifestation into reality.

Say:

"By earth, air, fire, and sea, bring my desires to life, let them be. Balance of elements, scales now weigh, draw in abundance, manifest today. So mote it be."

Visualize your intentions glowing with light, carried into the universe by the combined energies of the elements. Trust that the forces you have summoned are now working to bring your desires into reality.

7. Concluding the Ritual

Gently blow out the candle, watching the smoke rise as a final offering to the universe. Allow the incense to burn down naturally, or wave the feather one last time to disperse the energy. Place the parchment and the crystal in a safe place, such as on your altar or a special drawer, to keep the energy of your manifestation active.

8. Reflecting on the Ritual

Sit quietly for a few moments, feeling the balanced energy of the elements surrounding you. Open your journal and write down your experience, including the intentions you set, the emotions you felt, and any insights that arose during the ritual. In the days and weeks following, observe how your desires begin to manifest in your life and how the balanced energy you created continues to support your goals.

Tips for Enhancing Manifestation

- **Daily Affirmations:** Hold the crystal each morning and repeat a positive affirmation, such as "I am aligned with the elements; my desires manifest with ease."
- **Regular Elemental Work:** Spend time outdoors connecting with the elements—walking barefoot (earth), deep breathing (air), candle meditations (fire), and spending time near water (water)—to maintain a balanced flow of energy.
- **Revisit Your Intentions:** Check in with your written intentions periodically and adjust them as needed, ensuring that they remain in harmony with your current path.

Final Thoughts

The "Scales of Creation: Manifestation Spell" is a powerful ritual that draws upon the balanced energies of earth, air, fire, and water to bring your desires into reality. By working with each element, you create a harmonious space where your intentions can grow and take shape. This spell aligns with Libra's need for equilibrium, ensuring that your manifestations are not just driven by desire but are also grounded, thoughtful, and nurtured.

Manifestation is not just about calling in what you want; it's about aligning your thoughts, emotions, and actions with the universe's energy in a balanced way. As you work with this spell, let it remind you of the beauty of harmony and the power of the elements to support your dreams. With balanced intention and the energy of the elements at your side, you hold the power to bring your desires into existence, creating a life that reflects your truest self

Appendices
Appendix A: Libran Star Chart

In astrology, the stars, planets, and celestial events play a crucial role in shaping the energies and influences that affect our lives. As a Libra, ruled by Venus, your connection to the cosmos is especially tied to harmony, balance, love, and beauty. Your star chart is a celestial map that reveals how various planetary positions and cosmic events affect you, particularly in relation to spellwork and manifestation. This appendix provides an in-depth guide to the key celestial influences for Libras, including ruling planets, important zodiac constellations, and specific celestial events that can enhance or influence your magical practices.

A well-crafted star chart serves as a valuable reference when performing spellwork, allowing you to time your rituals with the most supportive planetary energies. The influence of Venus, lunar cycles, eclipses, retrogrades, and specific planetary alignments can amplify the effectiveness of your intentions, spellwork, and manifestation efforts. This chart will help you understand when to harness these cosmic energies to maximize the outcomes of your magical practices.

Overview of Libra in Astrology

Symbol: The Scales

Element: Air

Modality: Cardinal

Ruling Planet: Venus

House: Seventh House (Relationships, Partnerships, Balance)

Key Traits: Harmony, Balance, Fairness, Diplomacy, Aesthetics

As a cardinal air sign, Libra is the initiator of balance and harmony. Governed by Venus, the planet of love, beauty, and attraction, Libras possess a natural affinity for creating peaceful environments and fostering relationships. In spellwork, this affinity can be harnessed to promote love, beauty, balance, justice, and harmony.

Libra's Ruling Planet: Venus

Venus, the brightest planet in the night sky, is the ruler of Libra and greatly influences your energy and magical abilities. Venus embodies love, beauty, pleasure, art, and luxury, making it the most favorable planet for spells related to romance, self-care, beauty, creativity, and financial prosperity. Here's how Venus affects spellwork:

- **Venus Retrograde:** This occurs approximately every 18 months and lasts for about 40 days. During Venus retrograde, spellwork related to love, relationships, and finances may require extra care. This period is best suited for reflection, reassessment, and releasing old patterns rather than starting new romantic or financial endeavors.
- **Venus Direct:** When Venus is direct (not in retrograde), it's an optimal time for spellwork focused on love, attraction, beauty, financial abundance, and enhancing personal charm.
- **Venus Transits:** When Venus transits different zodiac signs, it brings a variety of influences. For Libras, Venus's transit through Libra (usually lasting about 3–4 weeks once a year) amplifies your natural charm, diplomacy, and attraction, making it an excellent time for spells focused on self-love, relationship harmony, and personal development.

Libra and the Moon Cycles

The moon's phases significantly affect Libran spellwork. As a sign that thrives on harmony and balance, Libras are particularly sensitive to the lunar cycle's influence on emotions, intuition, and energy levels. Here's how each moon phase can enhance your spellwork:

- **New Moon in Libra:** This phase is ideal for setting intentions related to relationships, harmony, and personal growth. It's the best time for spells that focus on new beginnings, particularly in love, partnership, and beauty.
- **First Quarter Moon in Libra:** A time for taking action toward your intentions and confronting obstacles that block your path to balance. Use this phase for spells that require courage, decision-making, and initiating changes.
- **Full Moon in Libra:** Occurs once a year, generally in March or April. This powerful phase amplifies energies associated with love, harmony, balance, and justice. Use it for manifestation spells, rituals that promote peace, and spells to strengthen relationships.
- **Last Quarter Moon in Libra:** Ideal for releasing any disharmony, emotional baggage, or negative energy within relationships. This phase supports spells focused on letting go, cutting cords, and seeking inner balance.

Important Celestial Events Influencing Libra Spellwork

Celestial events, such as planetary alignments, retrogrades, and eclipses, create powerful energy shifts that can enhance or challenge spellwork. Understanding these events can help you align your rituals with the most beneficial energies.

1. Venus Retrograde

- **Impact:** During this period, Libras may experience challenges in love, beauty, and financial matters. It is a time of reflection and re-assessment.
- **Best Spellwork:** Use this time for introspective spells, self-care rituals, and releasing unhealthy relationship patterns. Avoid starting new love spells or financial endeavors until Venus goes direct.

2. Mercury Retrograde

- **Impact:** Mercury retrograde can disrupt communication, technology, and travel, which can affect spellwork that requires precise communication, such as binding spells or agreements.
- **Best Spellwork:** Focus on spells that involve introspection, reflection, and revisiting past situations. Avoid spells that require new beginnings, clarity in communication, or intricate planning.

3. Solar and Lunar Eclipses

- **Solar Eclipse:** Brings powerful energy for transformation, especially in areas related to self-identity and personal goals. For Libras, solar eclipses can be an ideal time for spells focused on personal growth, empowerment, and initiating new paths.
- **Lunar Eclipse:** Intensifies emotions and reveals hidden truths. This is a potent time for Libras to perform spells for release, closure, and emotional healing, especially in relationships.

4. Venus-Jupiter Conjunction

- **Impact:** A rare and auspicious alignment of Venus and Jupiter that enhances love, abundance, and luck. For Libras, this conjunction amplifies charm, social success, and financial prosperity.
- **Best Spellwork:** Spells for love, beauty, wealth, and success are particularly powerful during this alignment.

5. Mars in Libra

- **Impact:** When Mars transits Libra, it brings energy and drive but may also introduce conflicts in relationships if not handled diplomatically.
- **Best Spellwork:** Use this time for spells that require assertiveness, courage, and action in creating balance. Be mindful to avoid overly aggressive or confrontational spellwork.

Libra's Star Constellation and Fixed Stars

The Libra constellation lies between Virgo and Scorpio and is associated with the scales of justice. While there are many stars within the constellation, a few fixed stars have a particular influence on Libras:

Zubenelgenubi and Zubeneschamali

- **Zubenelgenubi (Alpha Librae):** Known as the "Southern Scale," it symbolizes balance, justice, and fairness. This star's influence is perfect for spellwork that seeks to restore harmony, resolve conflicts, and make fair decisions.
- **Zubeneschamali (Beta Librae):** Known as the "Northern Scale," it is associated with intellect, success, and fortune. Spells performed under the influence of Zubeneschamali can be focused on intellectual pursuits, career success, and attracting positive opportunities.

Planetary Rulership and Their Influence on Libra's Spellwork

While Venus is Libra's ruling planet, other planetary influences also play a role in Libran spellwork, depending on their positions in the star chart.

- **Moon:** Governs emotions, intuition, and the subconscious. In Libra, the Moon enhances the emotional balance needed for self-care, love, and relationship spells.
- **Mercury:** Governs communication and intellect. When Mercury is in Libra, it enhances your ability to articulate intentions, making it an excellent time for spells involving agreements, negotiations, and clear communication.
- **Jupiter:** Represents expansion, luck, and abundance. When Jupiter transits Libra, it brings opportunities for growth, learning, and prosperity spells.
- **Saturn:** Governs discipline, structure, and boundaries. Saturn in Libra encourages spells related to setting boundaries, protection, and bringing structure to chaotic situations.

Using the Star Chart for Spell Timing

To harness the full potential of the celestial influences in your spellwork, refer to the following tips:

1. **New Moon in Libra:** Perform spells focused on new beginnings, setting intentions for balance in relationships, beauty, and self-love.
2. **Full Moon in Libra:** Manifestation spells for love, harmony, and success are most effective. Use this time for rituals that celebrate achievements and amplify positive energies.
3. **Venus Direct:** An optimal period for love spells, beauty rituals, and spells to attract wealth and abundance.

4. **Venus Retrograde:** Focus on introspective and self-care spells. Avoid initiating new relationships or financial ventures until Venus goes direct.
5. **Solar and Lunar Eclipses:** Embrace the transformative energies of eclipses for spells related to deep emotional healing, closure, and empowering changes.
6. **Mercury Retrograde:** Engage in spells for reflection, releasing past issues, and re-establishing inner harmony.

Final Thoughts on the Libran Star Chart

Understanding Libra's star chart is key to mastering the art of spell-work. By aligning your magical practices with the cosmic energies at play, you enhance your ability to manifest desires, achieve emotional balance, and maintain harmony in your life. Whether it's working with Venus's influence to attract love, using the moon's cycles for setting intentions, or harnessing the power of celestial events, your connection to the cosmos is an invaluable guide in your magical journey.

Let this star chart serve as a constant reminder of the cosmic forces that influence your life as a Libra. By embracing these celestial energies and working with them in harmony, you can enhance your spellwork and create a life filled with the balance, beauty, and love that defines your Libran essence.

Appendix B: Herbs and Crystals for Libra

Libras, ruled by Venus, are naturally drawn to beauty, harmony, and balance. In spellwork, herbs and crystals are essential tools that enhance intentions and amplify magical energy. For Libras, specific herbs and crystals resonate with their energy, helping to align their spellwork with their intrinsic qualities of love, justice, diplomacy, and aesthetic appreciation. This appendix provides a detailed guide to the herbs and crystals associated with Libra, their properties, and how to use them effectively in magical practices.

By incorporating these herbs and crystals into your spells, rituals, and daily practices, you can harness the balanced and harmonious energy that defines your Libra nature. Each herb and crystal listed here supports different aspects of Libra's magical and personal growth, whether it's enhancing relationships, finding inner balance, or attracting abundance.

Herbs for Libra

Libra is associated with fragrant, gentle, and balancing herbs that promote harmony, love, and beauty. Below is a comprehensive list of herbs commonly connected to Libra, along with their properties and uses in spellwork.

1. Rose

- **Properties:** Love, Beauty, Healing, Emotional Balance
- **Uses:** As one of the most prominent Venus-ruled plants, roses are perfect for spells involving love, beauty, self-care, and emotional healing. Use rose petals in love spells, beauty rituals, and self-love baths. Rose oil or water can also be used to anoint candles and charms for enhancing romantic attraction.

- **In Spellwork:** Sprinkle dried rose petals around candles during love or beauty spells to amplify the energy of Venus. Use rose water in cleansing rituals to promote self-love and emotional harmony.

2. Lavender

- **Properties:** Calmness, Peace, Balance, Cleansing
- **Uses:** Lavender's soothing energy helps bring calmness, balance, and peace to the mind and spirit. It is excellent for spells aimed at emotional healing, stress relief, and promoting restful sleep. Lavender can also be used in sachets for balance and tranquility.
- **In Spellwork:** Burn dried lavender as an incense to cleanse the space before beginning a spell. Add lavender buds to charm bags or bath rituals to promote inner peace and emotional balance.

3. Thyme

- **Properties:** Courage, Clarity, Purification
- **Uses:** Thyme is associated with courage and mental clarity, making it a useful herb for spells that require decisiveness and clear thinking. It also has purifying properties, helping to cleanse negative energy and promote a positive mindset.
- **In Spellwork:** Add dried thyme to purification rituals or burn it as an offering to clear away confusion and foster clarity before performing spellwork, especially for decision-making spells.

4. Catnip

- **Properties:** Attraction, Love, Happiness, Friendship
- **Uses:** Catnip's playful and loving energy is ideal for spells focused on attraction, happiness, and enhancing friendships. It is partic-

ularly effective in love spells and rituals for strengthening bonds with others.

- **In Spellwork:** Use catnip in charm bags for attracting new friendships or enhancing romantic connections. Add it to love sachets to draw positive attention and deepen emotional connections.

5. Chamomile

- **Properties:** Peace, Relaxation, Prosperity, Harmony
- **Uses:** Chamomile has a calming and peaceful energy, perfect for spells that seek to bring harmony into stressful situations or soothe emotional turbulence. It is also known for attracting prosperity and abundance.
- **In Spellwork:** Brew chamomile tea for use in relaxation rituals or prosperity spells. Sprinkle dried chamomile around your space during rituals to promote peace and attract gentle, harmonious energy.

6. Violet

- **Properties:** Tranquility, Love, Protection, Healing
- **Uses:** Violets are associated with protection, love, and emotional healing. Their gentle energy helps to soothe tensions in relationships and promote inner tranquility.
- **In Spellwork:** Place dried violet petals in sachets for love and protection. Use violet oil to anoint candles in rituals aimed at emotional healing and fostering a sense of calm.

7. Yarrow

- **Properties:** Courage, Protection, Balance, Clarity
- **Uses:** Yarrow promotes courage and emotional balance, helping Libras to make decisions and protect their energies. It is also used for enhancing psychic abilities and promoting mental clarity.
- **In Spellwork:** Carry yarrow in a charm bag for protection and inner strength. Add it to baths for enhancing courage and emotional fortitude.

Crystals for Libra

Crystals that resonate with Libra are those that promote harmony, love, balance, and mental clarity. Here is a detailed list of crystals aligned with Libra energy, their properties, and their uses in spellwork.

1. Rose Quartz

- **Properties:** Unconditional Love, Emotional Healing, Self-Love, Compassion
- **Uses:** Rose quartz is the quintessential love stone, ruled by Venus. It opens the heart chakra, fostering unconditional love, self-love, and emotional healing. This crystal is ideal for love spells, relationship harmony, and self-care rituals.
- **In Spellwork:** Place rose quartz on your altar during love spells or carry it as a charm to attract loving energy. Use it in self-love baths to promote feelings of worthiness and compassion.

2. Lapis Lazuli

- **Properties:** Wisdom, Clarity, Truth, Balance
- **Uses:** Lapis lazuli is associated with wisdom, truth, and mental clarity. It helps Libras navigate their thoughts and make decisions based on balance and fairness. This crystal also enhances communication and self-expression.
- **In Spellwork:** Meditate with lapis lazuli before performing spells that require insight and truth. Use it in rituals to enhance clarity in communication, especially during spells for resolving conflicts or making decisions.

3. Amethyst

- **Properties:** Calmness, Intuition, Protection, Balance
- **Uses:** Amethyst is known for its soothing and balancing energy. It calms the mind, enhances intuition, and provides spiritual protection. Amethyst is excellent for meditation, stress relief, and spells related to emotional healing and balance.
- **In Spellwork:** Place amethyst on your altar during meditation rituals to promote mental clarity and spiritual insight. Use it in protective spells to shield your emotional energy.

4. Green Aventurine

- **Properties:** Luck, Prosperity, Harmony, Growth
- **Uses:** Known as the "Stone of Opportunity," green aventurine attracts luck, prosperity, and positive energy. It encourages personal growth and emotional healing, helping Libras maintain balance in their lives.
- **In Spellwork:** Use green aventurine in prosperity spells to attract wealth and abundance. Place it in your workspace to enhance luck and opportunities in career-related pursuits.

5. Clear Quartz

- **Properties:** Clarity, Amplification, Healing, Energy Balance
- **Uses:** Clear quartz is a versatile crystal that amplifies intentions and energy. It enhances mental clarity, promotes balance, and can be used in any spell to amplify the energy of other crystals and herbs.
- **In Spellwork:** Incorporate clear quartz in spell jars or grids to boost the energy of your intentions. Use it in meditation to clear mental fog and enhance focus.

6. Citrine

- **Properties:** Joy, Abundance, Confidence, Manifestation
- **Uses:** Citrine is associated with joy, confidence, and manifestation. It is a powerful stone for attracting prosperity, enhancing self-esteem, and promoting positive energy in spellwork.
- **In Spellwork:** Use citrine in abundance and manifestation rituals to attract wealth and success. Carry it as a charm for confidence and to maintain an optimistic mindset.

7. Blue Lace Agate

- **Properties:** Communication, Calmness, Emotional Healing, Balance
- **Uses:** Blue lace agate enhances communication, calmness, and emotional healing. It is especially helpful for Libras who seek to express their thoughts with clarity and diplomacy.
- **In Spellwork:** Wear or carry blue lace agate during conversations or negotiations to promote clear, calm communication. Use it in spells for emotional balance and soothing anxiety.

How to Use Herbs and Crystals in Libra Spellwork

- **Herbal Sachets:** Create herbal sachets using Libra-associated herbs (such as rose, lavender, and catnip) to carry in your bag, place under your pillow, or keep on your altar. These sachets can be customized for specific intentions, like love, balance, or protection.
- **Crystal Grids:** Arrange a crystal grid with Libra-related crystals like rose quartz, amethyst, and citrine to amplify your intentions during rituals. Place the grid in a prominent area where you perform spellwork.

- **Candle Dressing:** Dress candles with herbal oils (such as lavender or rose oil) and sprinkle dried herbs around them for spells focused on love, harmony, and beauty.
- **Bath Rituals:** Incorporate herbs like chamomile, rose petals, and lavender into bath rituals for self-care and emotional healing. Add crystals like rose quartz or amethyst to the bath to amplify the soothing energies.
- **Crystal Meditation:** Meditate with Libra-associated crystals to align your energy before spellwork, enhancing focus, balance, and clarity.

Final Thoughts on Herbs and Crystals for Libra

Herbs and crystals are powerful allies in spellwork, especially for Libras who seek harmony, balance, and love in all aspects of life. By understanding and utilizing the unique properties of these natural elements, you can enhance your rituals, align your energy with the cosmos, and bring your intentions to fruition. Let this guide serve as a trusted reference for choosing the right herbs and crystals to support your magical practices, ensuring that they resonate with your Libran nature and the energies you wish to cultivate.

Appendix C: Moon Phases and Their Influence

The moon, with its rhythmic cycles, plays a significant role in influencing emotions, energy, and intentions. For Libras, who seek harmony, balance, and inner peace, working with the moon's phases is an essential part of spellcasting. Each phase of the lunar cycle offers unique energies that align with various aspects of Libra's spellwork, from setting intentions and manifestation to release and self-reflection.

In this appendix, you'll find a detailed guide to how each moon phase influences Libra's spellcasting, along with specific rituals and practices tailored to enhance your magic during each phase. By timing your spells to correspond with the moon's energy, you can align your intentions with the natural flow of the universe, creating more potent and effective outcomes.

The Eight Moon Phases and Their Influence on Libra's Spellcasting

The lunar cycle consists of eight distinct phases, each offering specific energies that support different types of spells and rituals. As a Libra, you can harness these phases to cultivate balance, attract love, release negativity, and manifest your desires.

1. New Moon: Setting Intentions and New Beginnings

Influence: The New Moon represents new beginnings, fresh starts, and a blank slate. This is an ideal time for Libras to set intentions related to love, harmony, balance, and personal growth. The energy of the New Moon is quiet, introspective, and potent, making it perfect for spells focused on planting the seeds of future goals and desires.

Recommended Ritual: Intention-Setting Ritual for Harmony

- **Materials Needed:** A white candle, a piece of parchment, a green or pink pen, rose petals, and lavender oil.

- **Steps:**
  1. Light the white candle to symbolize the purity and potential of the new lunar cycle.
  2. Anoint the parchment with a drop of lavender oil to promote balance and calmness.
  3. Write down your intentions for the coming month, focusing on areas where you seek harmony, new love, or personal growth. Be specific in your wording.
  4. Sprinkle the rose petals over the parchment, saying: *"New Moon's light, pure and clear, I set my intentions, let balance draw near."*
  5. Place the parchment on your altar or under your pillow to allow your intentions to take root during the lunar cycle.

Best Spells for this Phase: New beginnings, love spells, self-improvement, setting intentions for balance.

2. Waxing Crescent: Building Energy and Attraction

Influence: The Waxing Crescent phase is when the moon begins to grow, symbolizing the accumulation of energy and momentum. For Libras, this phase is excellent for nurturing your intentions, building self-confidence, and attracting positive energy into your life. It's a time to solidify plans and take small, proactive steps toward your goals.

Recommended Ritual: Nurturing Growth Spell

- **Materials Needed:** A green candle, a bowl of soil, a small seed or crystal (e.g., rose quartz), and lavender.
- **Steps:**
  1. Light the green candle to symbolize growth and attraction.
  2. Hold the seed or crystal in your hands, infusing it with your intention for growth and positive change.
  3. Plant the seed in the soil or place the crystal in the bowl, saying: *"Crescent moon, waxing bright, nurture my dreams, with your light."*

4. Sprinkle lavender over the soil to promote peace and harmony as your intention grows.

5. Place the bowl in a sunny spot as a reminder to nurture your intentions daily.

Best Spells for this Phase: Attraction, confidence-building, love and friendship, goal-setting.

3. First Quarter: Taking Action and Overcoming Obstacles

Influence: The First Quarter moon marks a period of action, decision-making, and overcoming challenges. This is the time for Libras to address any obstacles that may be hindering their progress and to take decisive steps toward their goals. The energy of this phase is dynamic and assertive, helping to break free from stagnation.

Recommended Ritual: Obstacle-Removing Spell

- **Materials Needed:** A red candle, thyme, a piece of parchment, and a pen.
- **Steps:**
  1. Light the red candle, focusing on its flame as a symbol of courage and strength.
  2. Write down any obstacles or challenges that you are facing on the parchment.
  3. Sprinkle thyme over the parchment, saying: *"Quarter moon, bold and bright, give me strength, clear my sight. Remove these blocks, free my way, guide me forward, come what may."*
  4. Fold the parchment and hold it over the candle flame (safely) until the edges darken, visualizing the obstacles burning away.
  5. Bury the parchment in the soil as a symbol of transformation and growth.

Best Spells for this Phase: Overcoming challenges, breaking bad habits, courage, taking action.

4. Waxing Gibbous: Refinement and Adjustments

Influence: The Waxing Gibbous moon is a time for refining your intentions and making any necessary adjustments. The energy of this phase encourages Libras to reassess their progress and align their actions more closely with their goals. It's a period of perfecting plans and preparing for the culmination of efforts during the Full Moon.

Recommended Ritual: Intention-Refinement Ritual

- **Materials Needed:** A yellow candle, chamomile tea, a piece of parchment, and a pen.
- **Steps:**
  1. Light the yellow candle to promote clarity and insight.
  2. Brew chamomile tea and sip it slowly, allowing its calming properties to bring you into a state of reflection.
  3. Write down any adjustments or refinements you wish to make to your intentions.
  4. Hold the parchment near the candle flame and say: *"Gibbous moon, almost whole, refine my path, perfect my goal. With clear intent and focused mind, guide my way, let truth unwind."*
  5. Place the parchment on your altar as a reminder to stay aligned with your goals.

Best Spells for this Phase: Refinement, clarity, motivation, goal alignment.

5. Full Moon: Manifestation and Release

Influence: The Full Moon is the most powerful phase of the lunar cycle, representing peak energy and the culmination of your efforts. For Libras, this is an excellent time to manifest desires, celebrate achievements, and release anything that no longer serves you. The Full Moon's energy enhances spells related to love, balance, and harmony.

Recommended Ritual: Manifestation and Release Ritual

- **Materials Needed:** A white or silver candle, a small bowl of water, a piece of rose quartz, and a piece of parchment.
- **Steps:**
  1. Light the candle and place the rose quartz in the bowl of water to symbolize emotional clarity and the manifestation of your desires.
  2. Write down your manifestations on the parchment, being specific and positive.
  3. Hold the parchment over the candlelight and say: *"Full moon bright, shining light, manifest my dreams tonight. I release the old, embrace the new, by your power, my will comes true."*
  4. Dip your fingers in the water and sprinkle it around you to seal the energy of the ritual.
  5. Place the parchment under the bowl of water to infuse it with the Full Moon's energy overnight.

Best Spells for this Phase: Manifestation, release, emotional healing, celebrating achievements.

6. Waning Gibbous: Gratitude and Sharing Wisdom

Influence: After the Full Moon, the Waning Gibbous phase is a time for gratitude, reflection, and sharing the wisdom you have gained. This phase supports Libras in expressing gratitude for what they have manifested and in letting go of excess or negativity. It's a period for inner work and giving thanks.

Recommended Ritual: Gratitude and Release Spell

- **Materials Needed:** A pink candle, a bowl of saltwater, a rose petal, and a piece of parchment.
- **Steps:**
  1. Light the pink candle to symbolize gratitude and emotional healing.
  2. Write a list of things you are grateful for on the parchment.
  3. Place the rose petal in the bowl of saltwater, saying: *"Waning moon, gentle flow, I give thanks for all I know. Release the old, welcome peace, with gratitude, my heart finds ease."*
  4. Sprinkle a few drops of the saltwater around your space to clear any residual negativity.
  5. Keep the parchment as a reminder of your gratitude and blessings.

Best Spells for this Phase: Gratitude, sharing knowledge, reflection, emotional release.

7. Last Quarter: Letting Go and Breaking Patterns

Influence: The Last Quarter moon is the time for releasing and letting go of what no longer serves you. This phase encourages Libras to break free from old habits, emotional baggage, and anything that disrupts their balance. It's a period of introspection and renewal.

Recommended Ritual: Cord-Cutting and Letting Go Spell

- **Materials Needed:** A black candle, a small piece of string, scissors, and a piece of parchment.
- **Steps:**
  1. Light the black candle to represent release and transformation.
  2. Write down what you wish to let go of on the parchment.
  3. Tie a knot in the string, visualizing it as the negative energy or attachment you wish to release.
  4. Hold the string over the candle flame and say: *"Quarter moon, dark and deep, break these ties, my peace to keep. I cut this cord, I let it go, I release the past, in love I grow."*
  5. Use the scissors to cut the string, symbolizing the release of your burden.
  6. Bury the parchment and the cut string in the earth to complete the release.

Best Spells for this Phase: Releasing negativity, breaking bad habits, banishing spells, self-cleansing.

8. Waning Crescent: Rest and Reflection

Influence: The Waning Crescent is the final phase of the lunar cycle, representing rest, reflection, and preparation for new beginnings. This is the time for Libras to retreat inward, reflect on their journey, and recharge their energy. It's a period of deep inner peace and contemplation.

Recommended Ritual: Restorative Self-Care Ritual

- **Materials Needed:** A blue or white candle, chamomile tea, a piece of parchment, and a pen.
- **Steps:**
  1. Light the candle to symbolize peace and reflection.
  2. Brew a cup of chamomile tea, letting its calming scent fill your space.
  3. Sit quietly and reflect on your intentions from the past lunar cycle, noting any lessons learned or emotions that surface.
  4. Write down your thoughts and feelings on the parchment as a form of release and self-reflection.
  5. Sip the chamomile tea, allowing its soothing energy to replenish your spirit and prepare you for the new lunar cycle.

Best Spells for this Phase: Reflection, rest, self-care, deep inner work.

Final Thoughts on Moon Phases and Their Influence on Libra's Spellcasting

The moon's phases provide a natural rhythm that guides and supports your spellwork, helping you to align your intentions with the changing energies of the universe. As a Libra, working with the moon allows you to harness its cycles for balance, harmony, manifestation, and self-reflection. By timing your rituals to correspond with each moon phase, you can amplify your magic and bring your desires into alignment with the cosmos.

Let this guide serve as your lunar companion, helping you navigate the ebb and flow of the moon's energies and enhancing your spellcasting practices. With the moon as your ally, you have a powerful tool for creating a life that reflects your Libran ideals of beauty, balance, and harmony.

Appendix D: Glossary

This glossary provides definitions of key terms and concepts related to Libra, spellcraft, and astrology. Understanding these terms will enhance your knowledge of the subjects covered in this guide, providing clarity and insight into the various aspects of Libran spellwork and astrology. Use this glossary as a reference to deepen your comprehension of magical practices, astrological influences, and the unique qualities of Libra.

Air Element

- **Definition:** One of the four classical elements in astrology, representing intellect, communication, and thought. Libra, along with Gemini and Aquarius, is an air sign. Air element traits include curiosity, a love of learning, social interaction, and the ability to see multiple perspectives.
- **Relevance:** In spellcraft, the air element governs spells related to communication, clarity, and mental focus. Libras often work with the air element to enhance intellectual pursuits and promote harmonious interactions.

Altar

- **Definition:** A designated space where magical and spiritual activities are performed. An altar usually holds items that represent the four elements (earth, air, fire, water), candles, crystals, herbs, and symbols relevant to the practitioner's intentions.
- **Relevance:** In Libra spellwork, an altar is used to create a balanced and sacred space for rituals. Incorporating symbols of harmony, beauty, and love can strengthen the intentions set during spellcasting.

Amulet

- **Definition:** An object worn or carried for protection and to ward off negative energy. Amulets often contain symbols, crystals, or herbs with protective properties.
- **Relevance:** Libras can use amulets crafted with crystals like amethyst or rose quartz for protection and to maintain emotional balance. These amulets can be worn during spellwork or kept nearby for ongoing influence.

Astrology

- **Definition:** The study of the movements and relative positions of celestial bodies and their influence on human affairs and natural phenomena. Astrology uses the positions of the planets, the sun, and the moon to understand personality traits, life events, and cosmic energies.
- **Relevance:** For Libras, astrology provides insight into personal characteristics, relationships, and the timing of spellwork. By understanding the influence of their ruling planet Venus and other celestial bodies, Libras can align their spells with the cosmos for more powerful results.

Balance

- **Definition:** A state of equilibrium and harmony between opposing forces. In both mundane life and magic, balance involves creating a sense of proportion and steadiness.
- **Relevance:** Balance is a core concept for Libra, symbolized by the scales. In spellcraft, maintaining balance between elements, intentions, and energies is crucial for successful outcomes. Libras often

perform spells to restore emotional, spiritual, or relational balance.

Binding Spell

- **Definition:** A spell designed to restrict or contain a person, situation, or energy. Binding spells are often used to prevent harm, halt negative behavior, or protect oneself from external influences.
- **Relevance:** For Libras, binding spells are a way to protect their interests and maintain harmony in their lives. A binding spell may involve knotting a ribbon or using a representation of the situation to secure it from causing disruption.

Cardinal Sign

- **Definition:** One of the three astrological qualities, cardinal signs (Aries, Cancer, Libra, and Capricorn) mark the start of each season and are characterized by their initiating, dynamic, and leadership qualities.
- **Relevance:** As a cardinal sign, Libra has a natural ability to initiate balance, harmony, and new endeavors, especially in relationships. This quality makes Libras effective in performing spells that seek to start new cycles or restore equilibrium.

Chakra

- **Definition:** Energy centers within the body that correspond to different physical, emotional, and spiritual aspects. There are seven main chakras, each associated with a specific color, element, and function.
- **Relevance:** For Libras, the Heart Chakra (Anahata) is particularly significant as it relates to love, balance, and relationships.

Incorporating chakra alignment into spellwork can enhance emotional harmony and personal well-being.

Cleansing

- **Definition:** The act of purifying a space, object, or individual to remove negative or stagnant energy. Cleansing can involve various methods, such as smudging with herbs, using saltwater, or visualization.
- **Relevance:** Cleansing is a vital practice in Libra's spellcraft to maintain a balanced energy flow. Before any ritual, Libras often cleanse their space, tools, and themselves to create an environment of clarity and positivity.

Conjunction

- **Definition:** In astrology, a conjunction occurs when two or more planets align in the same sign or degree. This aspect typically enhances or intensifies the energies of the planets involved.
- **Relevance:** Conjunctions involving Venus (Libra's ruling planet) can significantly influence spellwork related to love, beauty, and relationships. For example, a Venus-Jupiter conjunction can amplify the energy of love spells, making them more effective.

Crystal Grid

- **Definition:** An arrangement of crystals in a geometric pattern to focus and amplify energy for specific intentions. Crystal grids often incorporate sacred geometry and are placed on an altar or sacred space.
- **Relevance:** Libras can create crystal grids using stones like rose quartz, amethyst, and clear quartz to enhance spells for harmony,

love, and emotional balance. The grid's structure allows Libras to direct and concentrate their energy on their desired outcome.

Divination

- **Definition:** The practice of seeking knowledge or insight into the future or unknown through various methods, such as tarot cards, astrology, pendulums, or scrying.
- **Relevance:** Libras can use divination to gain clarity and guidance before performing spells, particularly when making decisions about relationships, balance, or personal growth. Tarot readings can reveal the best timing and approach for spellwork.

Elemental Magic

- **Definition:** Magic that involves working with the four classical elements—earth, air, fire, and water—to enhance spells and rituals. Each element corresponds to different aspects of life and energy.
- **Relevance:** As an air sign, Libra is naturally attuned to the element of air, which governs intellect, communication, and clarity. In spellwork, Libras often incorporate elements like incense (air), candles (fire), water, and crystals (earth) to create a balanced ritual environment.

Equinox

- **Definition:** An astronomical event that occurs twice a year, when day and night are of equal length. The Spring (Vernal) and Autumn Equinoxes mark the start of Libra's season (Autumn).
- **Relevance:** The Autumn Equinox, associated with Libra, is a time of balance between light and darkness. Libras can harness

this energy for spellwork focused on equilibrium, transitions, and giving thanks for the abundance in life.

Full Moon

- **Definition:** The phase of the moon when it is fully illuminated by the sun, representing completion, manifestation, and the peak of energy.
- **Relevance:** The Full Moon in Libra is a powerful time for spells involving love, harmony, manifestation, and relationship healing. It is an optimal period for rituals that celebrate achievements and release negative energy.

Herbalism

- **Definition:** The practice of using plants and herbs for healing, spellwork, and magical purposes. Each herb has unique properties that can enhance specific types of magic.
- **Relevance:** Libras use herbs like rose, lavender, chamomile, and violet in spellcraft to promote love, balance, peace, and beauty. Herbal infusions, oils, and sachets are common tools in Libra's magical practices.

Intention

- **Definition:** The focused thought or desire behind a spell or ritual. Intention directs the energy in spellwork toward achieving a specific outcome.
- **Relevance:** Clear intention is essential in Libran spellwork, as it aligns the mind and heart with the desired goal. Libras often set intentions related to love, harmony, justice, and personal growth.

Knot Magic

- **Definition:** A form of magic that involves tying knots to bind, release, or set intentions. The number of knots and the type of cord used can influence the spell's outcome.
- **Relevance:** Libras use knot magic in binding spells to protect their interests and maintain harmony. By knotting a ribbon or cord, they can secure their intentions, whether it is for love, balance, or protection.

Lunar Cycle

- **Definition:** The progression of the moon through its phases, including the New Moon, Waxing Crescent, First Quarter, Waxing Gibbous, Full Moon, Waning Gibbous, Last Quarter, and Waning Crescent.
- **Relevance:** The lunar cycle greatly influences Libra's spellcasting. Each phase offers specific energies for different types of magic, such as setting intentions during the New Moon, refining spells during the Waxing Gibbous, and manifesting desires at the Full Moon.

Manifestation

- **Definition:** The process of bringing desires, goals, or intentions into reality through focused thought, energy, and action.
- **Relevance:** Libras often work with the moon's phases, elements, and crystals to manifest their desires. They use spells to attract love, beauty, abundance, and harmony into their lives by aligning their intentions with the universe's natural flow.

New Moon

- **Definition:** The phase of the moon when it is not visible from Earth, marking the beginning of the lunar cycle and symbolizing new beginnings and fresh starts.
- **Relevance:** The New Moon is an ideal time for Libras to set intentions for balance, love, and growth. It supports spells focused on initiating new projects, relationships, and personal changes.

Retrograde

- **Definition:** An apparent backward motion of a planet in the sky, which in astrology is believed to affect the areas of life that the planet governs.
- **Relevance:** Venus retrograde significantly affects Libras, as it influences love, relationships, and self-worth. During this period, Libras often focus on introspective spells and rituals for self-care, reflection, and healing.

Ruling Planet

- **Definition:** The planet that governs an astrological sign, imbuing it with its qualities and influencing its behavior and characteristics.
- **Relevance:** Venus is the ruling planet of Libra, embodying beauty, love, harmony, and balance. Understanding Venus's movements, retrogrades, and transits helps Libras time their spells for maximum effectiveness, especially in areas of love, attraction, and relationship healing.

Sigil

- **Definition:** A symbol created using letters, shapes, or imagery to represent a specific intention or desire in magic. Sigils are charged with energy and used as focal points during spellwork.
- **Relevance:** Libras can design sigils to represent their intentions, such as harmony, love, or justice, and use them in spells to focus their energy. These symbols can be drawn on parchment, carved into candles, or incorporated into ritual tools.

Smudging

- **Definition:** The practice of burning herbs, such as sage or lavender, to cleanse a space, object, or person of negative energy.
- **Relevance:** Smudging is an essential cleansing practice in Libra's spellwork, often performed before rituals to purify the space and promote a peaceful, balanced environment.

Waning Moon

- **Definition:** The phase of the moon following the Full Moon, during which the moon appears to decrease in size, representing a time of release, letting go, and introspection.
- **Relevance:** During the Waning Moon, Libras focus on spells for releasing negativity, breaking bad habits, and clearing emotional or spiritual clutter. It is an optimal time for self-care and healing.

Waxing Moon

- **Definition:** The phase of the moon from the New Moon to the Full Moon, during which the moon appears to grow larger, symbolizing growth, attraction, and building energy.

- **Relevance:** The Waxing Moon is a time for Libras to perform spells that nurture new intentions, attract positive energy, and build momentum toward their goals, such as love, success, and personal development.

Final Thoughts on the Glossary

This glossary covers a wide range of terms and concepts relevant to Libra's spellwork, astrology, and magic. By familiarizing yourself with these definitions, you deepen your understanding of the practices and influences that shape your magical journey. Use this glossary as a reference to navigate the complexities of spellcraft, the cosmos, and your unique Libran energy. With this knowledge, you can craft spells and rituals that resonate with your goals, align with the cosmic forces, and bring harmony and balance into your life.

Appendix E: Charts

In astrology, star charts (or natal charts) serve as celestial maps, revealing the positions of the planets, the sun, and the moon at a given time, usually at the moment of a person's birth. For Libras, these charts offer key insights into how Venus, the ruling planet, influences different aspects of life. This appendix provides a detailed star chart for Libra, outlining the role of Venus, its placement, and the significant celestial events that affect Libra's energy and spellwork. By understanding these celestial influences, Libras can harness astrological timing to enhance their rituals, spellcasting, and personal growth.

Below, you will find detailed information about the placement of Venus in Libra, how other celestial events such as planetary transits, retrogrades, and lunar cycles affect Libra, and how to use these events for optimal spellcasting. This star chart is designed to be a practical guide, helping you to align your magical practices with the cosmic energies that govern your zodiac sign.

Libra Star Chart: Key Components

1. **Ruling Planet:** Venus
2. **Element:** Air
3. **Modality:** Cardinal
4. **House:** Seventh House (Relationships, Partnerships, Harmony)
5. **Best Time for Spellcasting:** When Venus is in Libra or during Venus transits through harmonious signs (Taurus, Pisces).
6. **Challenging Times:** Venus Retrograde, Mercury Retrograde, Lunar Eclipses in Libra.

Section 1: Venus in Libra – Ruling Planet and Its Influence

Venus is the ruling planet of Libra, governing love, beauty, harmony, relationships, and aesthetic pleasures. It plays a dominant role in shaping the Libran approach to life and spellwork, particularly in areas related to romance, partnership, self-care, and artistic expression. Below is a breakdown of how Venus in Libra influences your star chart:

1. Venus in Libra (Natal Chart Placement)

- **Characteristics:** When Venus is in Libra in a natal chart, it emphasizes a natural inclination toward love, relationships, and creating harmony in one's surroundings. Individuals with this placement often seek balance and equality in partnerships and have a keen eye for beauty and aesthetics.
- **In Spellwork:** Libras with Venus in their sign can use this energy to amplify spells related to attracting love, enhancing self-beauty, and fostering harmony in relationships. Rituals for peace, fairness, and creative inspiration are particularly effective when Venus is strong in the natal chart.

2. Venus Transits and Their Influence on Spellwork

- **Venus in Libra:** When Venus transits through Libra (typically once a year for about 3-4 weeks), it marks a period of heightened charm, diplomacy, and attractiveness. This is the most auspicious time for Libras to perform love spells, beauty rituals, and spells aimed at creating harmony in relationships. Spells cast during this transit are empowered by the planet's energy, often leading to faster and more favorable outcomes.
- **Venus in Taurus or Pisces:** These transits are also favorable for Libras, as Venus is in its domicile in Taurus and exalted in Pisces, providing a supportive energy for spells related to romance, self-worth, creativity, and prosperity.

3. Venus Retrograde

- **Overview:** Venus retrograde occurs approximately every 18 months and lasts for about 40 days. During this period, the energies associated with Venus—love, beauty, relationships, and finances—are turned inward, creating a time of introspection and reassessment.
- **Effects on Libra:** Libras may find their relationships, self-perception, and aesthetic desires in flux. It is a challenging time for initiating new romantic endeavors, making significant financial investments, or performing attraction spells.
- **Best Spellwork:** During Venus retrograde, focus on introspective and self-healing spells. Rituals aimed at releasing old relationship patterns, self-love, and personal care are most effective.

Section 2: Lunar Influences on Libra

The moon's phases greatly affect the energy available for spellwork, particularly in Libra, a sign naturally attuned to balance and harmony. Each phase of the lunar cycle presents unique opportunities for Libras to align their magic with the moon's shifting energy.

1. New Moon in Libra

- **Energy:** New beginnings, setting intentions, planting seeds for future growth.
- **Recommended Spellwork:** Ideal for spells that seek to establish harmony, balance, and new relationships. This is the time to focus on setting intentions related to personal growth, love, and creative projects.
- **Astrological Timing:** This phase usually occurs in September or October, depending on the year. It's the perfect time to initiate projects or relationships that embody Libran qualities of peace, beauty, and fairness.

2. Full Moon in Libra

- **Energy:** Amplification, manifestation, and culmination of energies set during the New Moon.
- **Recommended Spellwork:** Best suited for spells related to love, emotional balance, and the completion of goals. Use this time to manifest desires, strengthen romantic bonds, and celebrate achievements.
- **Astrological Timing:** Typically occurs six months after the New Moon in Libra, around March or April. This full moon is especially potent for Libras, enhancing spellwork that aims to bring harmony and resolution to ongoing issues.

3. Lunar Eclipses in Libra

- **Energy:** Sudden shifts, revelations, and transformative changes.
- **Effects on Libra:** Lunar eclipses can bring about intense emotional experiences and shake up established relationships. They mark a period of release and necessary change.
- **Best Spellwork:** Focus on spells that aid in letting go, emotional healing, and transforming aspects of life that have become unbalanced. Avoid starting new ventures during this time; instead, use the eclipse energy for closure and preparation for new cycles.

Section 3: Planetary Transits and Aspects Affecting Libra
1. Mercury in Libra

- **Energy:** Enhanced communication, intellectual balance, diplomacy.
- **Recommended Spellwork:** Spells related to negotiation, communication, and clarity in relationships. It is an excellent time for Libras to write affirmations, create sigils, and perform rituals aimed at improving communication.

- **Challenges:** During Mercury retrograde in Libra, misunderstandings and miscommunications can arise. Avoid starting new agreements or spells that require precise outcomes during this time.

2. Mars in Libra

- **Energy:** Drive, courage, assertiveness in relationships, and balance of personal desires.
- **Effects on Spellwork:** Mars' transit through Libra can provide the energy needed to take action in relationships and creative projects. Spells that require courage, passion, or direct action benefit from this transit.
- **Challenges:** The energy of Mars can sometimes disrupt Libra's natural inclination toward peace and diplomacy, potentially leading to conflicts. When performing spellwork, focus on balancing assertiveness with harmony to navigate this period effectively.

3. Jupiter in Libra

- **Energy:** Expansion, growth, opportunities in relationships, and the pursuit of justice.
- **Recommended Spellwork:** A favorable time for spells that aim to attract abundance, prosperity, and personal growth. Libras can use this transit to enhance spells for career advancement, creative inspiration, and finding balance in partnerships.
- **Best Practices:** Use the expansive energy of Jupiter to broaden your spiritual practices, initiate long-term goals, and work on spells that support personal development and self-improvement.

4. Saturn in Libra

- **Energy:** Structure, responsibility, commitment, and redefining boundaries in relationships.
- **Effects on Libra:** Saturn's influence can bring lessons in patience, discipline, and the need for setting boundaries. It may highlight areas where Libras need to establish firmer foundations in their relationships and personal lives.
- **Best Spellwork:** Focus on protection spells, boundary-setting rituals, and spells for long-term commitment and stability. Use this time to reinforce your personal space and ensure that your relationships align with your values.

Section 4: Optimal Timing for Libra Spellcasting

The timing of spellwork is crucial for Libras, who seek to align their intentions with the most favorable cosmic energies. Here is a summarized chart for quick reference:

Celestial Event	Ideal Spellwork	Notes
Venus in Libra	Love, Beauty, Harmony, Attraction	Best time for love and self-care spells.
Venus Retrograde	Self-Reflection, Release, Self-Healing	Avoid initiating new romantic endeavors.
New Moon in Libra	New Beginnings, Harmony, Balance	Set intentions for the upcoming lunar cycle.
Full Moon in Libra	Manifestation, Relationship Healing	Focus on culmination and celebrating success.

Celestial Event	Ideal Spellwork	Notes
Mercury Retrograde	Reflection, Re-assessing Communication	Avoid spells requiring precise outcomes.
Lunar Eclipse in Libra	Release, Transformation, Emotional Healing	Focus on closure and inner transformation.
Jupiter in Libra	Abundance, Growth, Prosperity	Expand spellwork for personal development.
Saturn in Libra	Protection, Boundaries, Stability	Reinforce spells for long-term commitment.

Final Thoughts on Libra's Star Chart

The celestial events and planetary placements outlined in this star chart provide a detailed roadmap for Libras to navigate their magical practices effectively. By understanding the influence of Venus, lunar phases, and planetary transits, Libras can align their spellwork with the most supportive cosmic energies. Whether you are manifesting love, seeking balance, or undergoing a period of transformation, this star chart serves as a valuable reference for timing your rituals and harnessing the power of the universe in your spellcraft.

Let this chart be your guide as you work in harmony with the stars, weaving the energies of Venus, the moon, and other celestial bodies into your magic. With careful timing and a deep connection to the cosmic forces, you can create a life filled with balance, beauty, and love.

Chart 2: **Herbs: A Detailed Chart of Libra-Associated Herbs**

Libra, ruled by Venus, is associated with herbs that promote harmony, love, balance, beauty, and relaxation. The energy of these plants aligns with Libra's natural desire for peace and equilibrium, making them ideal for use in various spells, rituals, and daily practices. This detailed chart provides an overview of the most potent Libra-associated herbs, including their magical properties and practical uses in spellcraft.

The following chart lists a variety of herbs connected to Libra, describing their magical properties and offering suggestions on how to incorporate them into your spellwork. By using these herbs, Libras can enhance their magic, promote inner balance, attract love, and cultivate beauty in their lives.

Herb	Properties	Uses in Spell-craft	Additional Notes
Rose	Love, Beauty, Emotional Healing, Harmony	- Use rose petals in love spells, self-love rituals, and bath rituals to promote feelings of self-worth and attraction. - Add rose oil to candles during rituals for love and beauty. - Place dried rose petals in sachets for attracting love or strengthening romantic bonds.	Roses, ruled by Venus, resonate deeply with Libras. They can be added to altar spaces to amplify the energy of beauty and love.

Herb	Properties	Uses in Spell-craft	Additional Notes
Chamomile	Peace, Relaxation, Prosperity, Harmony	- Brew chamomile tea for calming and grounding before performing spells. - Add dried chamomile to sleep sachets to promote restful sleep and balance. - Incorporate chamomile in prosperity spells to attract abundance and luck.	Chamomile's soothing properties help Libras maintain emotional equilibrium and reduce stress.

Herb	Properties	Uses in Spellcraft	Additional Notes
Lavender	Calmness, Peace, Balance, Purification	- Burn lavender as an incense to cleanse and purify the space before rituals. - Use lavender oil in self-care rituals to promote relaxation and mental clarity. - Include lavender in charm bags for protection and emotional balance.	Lavender is excellent for reducing anxiety and creating a serene atmosphere for Libra's spellwork.

Herb	Properties	Uses in Spellcraft	Additional Notes
Mint	Clarity, Healing, Prosperity, Protection	- Add fresh mint to spell jars or sachets for mental clarity and focus. - Use mint leaves in abundance spells to attract wealth and success. - Brew mint tea to aid in emotional healing and refresh the spirit.	Mint has a refreshing energy that can help Libra clear their mind and stay focused on their intentions.
Thyme	Courage, Clarity, Purification, Healing	- Add dried thyme to purification rituals to cleanse spaces of negative energy. - Carry a sprig of thyme to enhance courage when facing difficult situations. - Use thyme in rituals for physical and emotional healing.	Thyme's energy supports Libras in overcoming indecision and finding the strength to act.

Herb	Properties	Uses in Spellcraft	Additional Notes
Catnip	Attraction, Love, Happiness, Friendship	- Include catnip in charm bags for attracting new friendships or deepening romantic connections. - Add to love spells to increase the playful and joyful energy in relationships. - Use in dream pillows to invite pleasant dreams and restful sleep.	Catnip's playful energy is particularly useful for Libras looking to enhance joy and love in their lives.

Herb	Properties	Uses in Spell-craft	Additional Notes
Violet	Tranquility, Love, Protection, Healing	- Place dried violet petals in sachets for protection, self-love, and emotional healing. - Anoint violet oil on candles during spells for peace and harmony. - Use violet in bath rituals to soothe tensions and promote self-acceptance.	Violets help Libras connect with their inner emotions and cultivate self-care practices.

Herb	Properties	Uses in Spellcraft	Additional Notes
Yarrow	Courage, Protection, Balance, Clarity	- Add yarrow to baths to enhance emotional balance and fortitude. - Carry yarrow in a charm bag for protection against negative influences. - Use in spells for decision-making to gain clarity and confidence.	Yarrow's protective properties make it a powerful ally for Libras seeking to maintain balance and assertiveness.
Lemon Balm	Calmness, Emotional Healing, Clarity, Happiness	- Use lemon balm in tea or tinctures to calm nerves and reduce anxiety before rituals. - Add to spell jars for promoting joy, harmony, and emotional healing. - Use in bath rituals to cleanse and uplift the spirit.	Lemon balm's soothing energy aids Libras in navigating emotional fluctuations and maintaining inner peace.

Herb	Properties	Uses in Spellcraft	Additional Notes
Hibiscus	Love, Passion, Attraction, Beauty	- Incorporate dried hibiscus petals in love spells to enhance attraction and passion. - Add to bath rituals to promote beauty and self-confidence. - Use hibiscus tea in rituals to celebrate and strengthen romantic connections.	Hibiscus embodies the passionate side of Venus, enhancing spells related to love and physical attraction.

Herb	Properties	Uses in Spellcraft	Additional Notes
Jasmine	Love, Spiritual Awareness, Harmony, Dreams	- Burn jasmine incense during love spells to heighten attraction and spiritual connection. - Add dried jasmine flowers to dream pillows for enhancing intuition and promoting restful sleep. - Use jasmine oil in beauty spells to promote self-love and confidence.	Jasmine's sweet scent promotes a serene atmosphere and connects Libras to their inner desires and dreams.

Herb	Properties	Uses in Spellcraft	Additional Notes
Sage	Protection, Purification, Wisdom, Healing	- Burn sage for smudging to cleanse spaces, objects, and oneself before rituals. - Use sage leaves in spell jars for wisdom and guidance in decision-making. - Place sage in sachets for protection against negative energy and harmful influences.	Sage's purifying properties are essential for clearing energy and creating a balanced environment for Libra's magic.

Herb	Properties	Uses in Spellcraft	Additional Notes
Rosemary	Clarity, Protection, Memory, Healing	- Include rosemary in spells for mental clarity, focus, and memory enhancement. - Use in protective charm bags to ward off negative influences and create a peaceful aura. - Add rosemary to bath rituals for physical and emotional healing.	Rosemary's uplifting energy helps Libras maintain a clear mind and promotes spiritual protection.

Herb	Properties	Uses in Spell-craft	Additional Notes
Marjoram	Happiness, Peace, Protection, Love	- Use marjoram in spells for happiness and harmony in relationships. - Include in sachets for promoting a peaceful home environment. - Add marjoram to bath rituals to cleanse and comfort the spirit, enhancing self-love.	Marjoram supports Libras in creating a nurturing space filled with joy and balance.

Herb	Properties	Uses in Spellcraft	Additional Notes
Honeysuckle	Prosperity, Success, Love, Intuition	- Add honeysuckle to spells for attracting wealth and success. - Use in love spells to strengthen emotional bonds and open the heart to romance. - Incorporate in divination practices to enhance intuition and psychic abilities.	Honeysuckle's sweet energy promotes growth and prosperity, aligning with Libra's desire for abundance and love.

Tips for Using Libra-Associated Herbs in Spellcraft

- **Creating Sachets:** Combine a selection of Libra-associated herbs (such as rose, lavender, and chamomile) into a small pouch to carry with you or place under your pillow. These herbal sachets can be tailored to specific intentions, like promoting love, peace, or self-confidence.
- **Herbal Baths:** Add dried herbs like chamomile, rose, and lavender to a warm bath to create a relaxing, self-care ritual. Include a few drops of essential oils (e.g., rose oil or lavender oil) to amplify the soothing and balancing effects.
- **Altar Offerings:** Place fresh or dried herbs on your altar as offerings to Venus or other deities associated with love, harmony,

and beauty. This enhances the energies of your rituals and creates a harmonious space for spellwork.

- **Candle Dressing:** Anoint candles with herbal oils (such as rose or lavender oil) and sprinkle dried herbs around them before lighting. This practice amplifies the energy of your spells, aligning them with your intentions for love, balance, or protection.

Final Thoughts on Libra-Associated Herbs

The herbs listed in this chart resonate with Libra's intrinsic qualities of harmony, love, and balance. By incorporating these plants into your spellwork, you can enhance your magic and connect more deeply with the energies of your ruling planet, Venus. Whether you're seeking love, emotional healing, or inner peace, these herbs provide natural support for your magical practices. Use this chart as a guide to select the right herbs for your spells and rituals, creating a more balanced and fulfilling life in alignment with your Libra essence.

Chart 3: **Crystals: A Detailed Chart of Libra's Crystals**

Libra, governed by Venus, thrives on harmony, love, balance, and beauty. Crystals that resonate with Libran energy enhance spellwork, provide emotional support, and help attract love, peace, and prosperity. The right crystals can amplify a Libra's natural qualities, promoting inner equilibrium and aiding in personal growth. This chart provides an overview of Libra-associated crystals, highlighting their magical properties and how to use them in various rituals and daily practices.

Crystal Chart for Libra

Crystal	Properties	Uses in Spellcraft	Additional Notes
Rose Quartz	Unconditional Love, Emotional Healing, Self-Love, Compassion	- Use in love spells to attract or strengthen romantic relationships. - Incorporate in self-care rituals to promote feelings of self-worth and compassion. - Place under your pillow or on your altar to enhance self-love and emotional healing.	Rose quartz, ruled by Venus, resonates strongly with Libras, amplifying their capacity for love and harmony.

Crystal	Properties	Uses in Spellcraft	Additional Notes
Opal	Inspiration, Emotional Balance, Amplification, Beauty	- Use opal in spells for enhancing creativity, inspiration, and beauty. - Carry or wear opal to balance emotions and encourage self-expression. - Include in divination practices to enhance intuition and insight into relationships.	Opal reflects Libra's love for beauty and balance, enhancing spells related to emotional harmony and artistic pursuits.

Crystal	Properties	Uses in Spell-craft	Additional Notes
Jade	Prosperity, Luck, Emotional Healing, Balance	- Incorporate jade in prosperity spells to attract wealth, success, and good fortune. - Use in meditation to promote emotional healing and calmness. - Place on your altar to enhance spells focused on harmony and inner peace.	Jade's soothing energy aligns with Libra's quest for inner and outer balance, fostering a sense of well-being.

Crystal	Properties	Uses in Spell-craft	Additional Notes
Lapis Lazuli	Wisdom, Clarity, Truth, Communication	- Use lapis lazuli in spells that require clear communication and understanding. - Meditate with lapis to enhance mental clarity and insight. - Place on the throat chakra to improve honesty and self-expression.	Lapis lazuli supports Libras in decision-making, helping them see the truth in complex situations.

Crystal	Properties	Uses in Spell-craft	Additional Notes
Amethyst	Calmness, Intuition, Protection, Balance	- Use amethyst in meditation to calm the mind and enhance intuition. - Place under your pillow for restful sleep and spiritual protection. - Add to spells for emotional healing and maintaining inner peace.	Amethyst's calming energy helps Libras navigate emotional fluctuations, promoting a sense of serenity.

Crystal	Properties	Uses in Spellcraft	Additional Notes
Clear Quartz	Clarity, Amplification, Healing, Energy Balance	- Use clear quartz in spellwork to amplify intentions and boost the energy of other crystals. - Place on your altar to promote clarity and focus during rituals. - Carry as a talisman for maintaining balance and positive energy.	Clear quartz is a versatile stone that aligns with Libra's need for clarity and energy balance in all areas of life.

Crystal	Properties	Uses in Spellcraft	Additional Notes
Sodalite	Logic, Emotional Balance, Intuition, Communication	- Use sodalite in spells for emotional healing and enhancing rational thought. - Carry during conversations or negotiations to promote clear communication. - Meditate with sodalite to strengthen intuition and self-trust.	Sodalite's balancing qualities assist Libras in maintaining harmony between their logical and emotional selves.

Crystal	Properties	Uses in Spellcraft	Additional Notes
Aventurine (Green)	Luck, Prosperity, Growth, Healing	- Incorporate green aventurine in abundance spells to attract success and prosperity. - Place in your workspace to promote creativity and new opportunities. - Use in self-healing rituals to enhance emotional recovery and well being.	Aventurine's energy fosters growth and positivity, helping Libras pursue their goals with confidence.

Crystal	Properties	Uses in Spellcraft	Additional Notes
Blue Lace Agate	Communication, Calmness, Peace, Emotional Healing	- Use blue lace agate in spells to improve communication and foster peaceful interactions. - Meditate with this stone to calm anxiety and encourage emotional healing. - Place on the throat chakra to enhance self-expression.	Blue lace agate supports Libras in expressing themselves with clarity and calmness, promoting harmonious relationships.

Crystal	Properties	Uses in Spell-craft	Additional Notes
Carnelian	Courage, Passion, Creativity, Motivation	- Use carnelian in spells that require courage, determination, and motivation. - Place on your sacral chakra during meditation to boost creativity and confidence. - Include in rituals for self-empowerment and overcoming indecision.	Carnelian's fiery energy helps Libras take bold actions while maintaining a sense of balance.

Crystal	Properties	Uses in Spellcraft	Additional Notes
Fluorite	Focus, Clarity, Mental Order, Protection	- Use fluorite in spellwork for mental clarity and decision-making. - Place in your workspace to enhance focus and dispel negative energy. - Include in protection spells to shield against emotional overwhelm.	Fluorite supports Libras in organizing their thoughts, promoting clear thinking and balanced decision-making.

Crystal	Properties	Uses in Spellcraft	Additional Notes
Tourmaline (Pink)	Love, Emotional Healing, Protection, Self-Love	- Use pink tourmaline in self-love rituals to foster emotional healing and compassion. - Place on your heart chakra during meditation to release emotional blockages. - Include in spells for protection and nurturing in relationships.	Pink tourmaline's gentle energy aligns with Libra's need for love, balance, and emotional security.

Crystal	Properties	Uses in Spellcraft	Additional Notes
Hematite	Grounding, Balance, Protection, Strength	- Use hematite in grounding rituals to balance and center your energy. - Place in spell jars for protection and to ward off negative influences. - Wear hematite jewelry to maintain a balanced and grounded state of mind.	Hematite's grounding properties support Libras in staying balanced amidst life's fluctuations.

Crystal	Properties	Uses in Spellcraft	Additional Notes
Moonstone	Intuition, Emotional Balance, New Beginnings	- Use moonstone in spells for enhancing intuition and emotional insight. - Place under your pillow for dream work and connecting with the subconscious. - Include in rituals that focus on new beginnings, particularly during the New Moon.	Moonstone's calming influence helps Libras navigate their emotions and embrace change gracefully.

Crystal	Properties	Uses in Spell-craft	Additional Notes
Obsidian	Protection, Grounding, Clarity, Truth	- Use obsidian in protection spells to create a shield against negative energy. - Meditate with obsidian to reveal hidden truths and gain clarity. - Place on your altar for grounding and enhancing spiritual protection.	Obsidian's reflective nature encourages Libras to face their inner truths and maintain balance.

Tips for Using Libra's Crystals in Spellcraft

- **Meditation:** Hold a crystal, such as rose quartz or lapis lazuli, during meditation to align with its energy. This practice can help Libras connect with their inner selves, find clarity, and enhance self-love.
- **Crystal Grids:** Create a crystal grid using Libra-associated stones (e.g., rose quartz, jade, and amethyst) to amplify your intentions for love, harmony, or emotional healing. Place the grid in a sacred space where it can continuously radiate positive energy.
- **Candle Dressing:** Place crystals around candles during rituals to enhance the energy of your spells. For example, surround a pink candle with rose quartz for love spells, or use green aventurine with a green candle for prosperity spells.

- **Jewelry and Talismans:** Wear crystals such as jade, rose quartz, or opal as jewelry to carry their balancing and harmonizing energy throughout the day. Carrying crystals as talismans in pockets or bags also helps maintain emotional balance and attract positive energy.
- **Altar Placement:** Place crystals on your altar to enhance the energy of your ritual space. For example, place lapis lazuli or sodalite to promote clear communication, or use amethyst to create a calming, spiritual atmosphere.

Final Thoughts on Libra's Crystals

The crystals listed in this chart resonate with Libra's essence of harmony, beauty, love, and balance. By incorporating these stones into spellwork and daily routines, Libras can amplify their natural energies, attract positive influences, and maintain emotional equilibrium. Whether you seek love, prosperity, or inner peace, these crystals offer a powerful way to align with the energies of Venus and the universe. Use this chart as a guide to select the right crystals for your magical practices, enhancing your journey toward a life filled with beauty, balance, and self-love.

Appendix F: Book Recommendations

For those looking to delve deeper into astrology, spellcraft, and the unique energies of Libra, a thoughtfully curated selection of books can offer both foundational knowledge and advanced insights. Whether you are new to these topics or seeking to expand your current understanding, this list encompasses a variety of resources, from astrological guides to spellwork manuals. Each book has been chosen to resonate with Libra's affinity for harmony, balance, beauty, and spiritual exploration, providing further guidance and inspiration in your magical journey.

This appendix categorizes the recommendations into sections to help you find the books best suited to your interests: Astrology Basics, Libra-Specific Astrology, Spellcraft and Rituals, Crystals and Herbs, and Advanced Astrology. These books serve as invaluable resources for deepening your knowledge, refining your practices, and enhancing your connection to the energies of Libra.

Section 1: Astrology Basics
1. "Astrology for the Soul" by Jan Spiller

- **Overview:** This book offers a comprehensive look into the role of the moon's nodes in astrology, revealing how they influence your life path and soul growth. Spiller provides practical exercises for personal development based on your astrological chart.
- **Why It's Recommended:** Although not Libra-specific, this book provides foundational astrological knowledge that can help you understand Libra's placement in your natal chart and its influence on your life journey. It's an excellent starting point for learning how different celestial influences shape personal experiences.

2. "The Only Astrology Book You'll Ever Need" by Joanna Martine Woolfolk

- **Overview:** A comprehensive guide to astrology, covering sun signs, moon signs, ascendants, and the placement of planets in each sign. This book also includes how to cast and interpret a natal chart.
- **Why It's Recommended:** This book is an essential resource for understanding basic astrology. Its detailed explanations of planetary positions and aspects help Libras understand how their ruling planet, Venus, interacts with other celestial bodies.

3. "Astrology: Using the Wisdom of the Stars in Your Everyday Life" by Carole Taylor

- **Overview:** This beautifully illustrated guide explores the zodiac signs, planets, houses, and aspects, providing a holistic understanding of how astrology influences daily life.
- **Why It's Recommended:** This book's visually engaging approach makes complex astrological concepts accessible. Libras, who often appreciate aesthetically pleasing and balanced presentations, will find this book both informative and enjoyable.

Section 2: Libra-Specific Astrology
4. "Sun Signs & Past Lives: Your Soul's Evolutionary Path" by Bernie Ashman

- **Overview:** This book explores the connection between your sun sign and past lives, focusing on the karmic influences that shape your personality. It provides insights into how each zodiac sign, including Libra, can achieve spiritual growth.

- **Why It's Recommended:** For Libras seeking to explore their spiritual evolution, this book offers a unique perspective on how past life experiences influence their current personality and relationships. It provides a deeper understanding of Libra's quest for harmony and balance.

5. "Libra: The Art of Living Well and Finding Balance" by Joanna Martine Woolfolk

- **Overview:** A detailed exploration of Libra's personality, relationships, and approach to life. This book delves into how Libras interact with other signs and provides guidance on how to live in harmony with their Libran nature.
- **Why It's Recommended:** This book is a must-have for Libras who want to understand their sun sign on a deeper level. It covers topics like love, career, health, and spirituality, offering practical advice on how Libras can harness their strengths and navigate their challenges.

6. "Libra: Harness the Power of the Zodiac" by Stella Andromeda

- **Overview:** A modern guide to understanding the unique qualities and energies of Libra, offering advice on how to live in alignment with the sign's natural traits.
- **Why It's Recommended:** This book is an easy-to-read, concise exploration of Libra's personality, providing actionable insights on love, work, wellness, and spirituality. Its modern take makes it perfect for both beginners and experienced astrologers.

Section 3: Spellcraft and Rituals

7. "The Modern Witchcraft Spell Book: Your Complete Guide to Crafting and Casting Spells" by Skye Alexander

- **Overview:** A comprehensive guide to spellcraft, including spells for love, prosperity, protection, and more. The book covers how to use tools like candles, crystals, herbs, and moon phases in spellwork.
- **Why It's Recommended:** This book is an excellent resource for Libras who wish to explore spellcraft. It provides detailed instructions for creating balanced and harmonious rituals, aligning perfectly with Libra's natural inclination toward beauty and order in magical practices.

8. "Wicca: A Guide for the Solitary Practitioner" by Scott Cunningham

- **Overview:** An accessible introduction to Wicca and its practices, including spells, rituals, and the use of natural elements. The book emphasizes the importance of harmony with nature in magical work.
- **Why It's Recommended:** Libras who resonate with natural magic and the use of elements will find this guide invaluable. Cunningham's focus on the balance between the practitioner and the natural world aligns with Libra's need for harmony in both life and spellcraft.

9. "Llewellyn's Complete Book of Correspondences" by Sandra Kynes

- **Overview:** A comprehensive reference book listing correspondences for spells, rituals, and magical practices. It includes associations for herbs, crystals, colors, deities, elements, and more.
- **Why It's Recommended:** This book is a perfect reference for Libras who want to create balanced spells with carefully selected components. Its detailed listings help ensure that every aspect of a ritual aligns with Libra's intention for harmony and beauty.

Section 4: Crystals and Herbs
10. "The Crystal Bible" by Judy Hall

- **Overview:** An extensive guide to over 200 crystals, detailing their properties, uses in healing, and associations with zodiac signs.
- **Why It's Recommended:** This book is essential for Libras looking to work with crystals like rose quartz, opal, and jade. It offers detailed descriptions of each stone's energy, how to use them in spellwork, and their connections to different aspects of life.

11. "The Complete Guide to Crystal Chakra Healing: Energy Medicine for Mind, Body, and Spirit" by Philip Permutt

- **Overview:** A guide to using crystals for chakra healing, with a focus on balancing emotional, mental, and spiritual energies. The book includes instructions on crystal placement and meditation.
- **Why It's Recommended:** For Libras who seek balance in their energy centers, this book provides practical guidance on using crystals to achieve equilibrium in mind, body, and spirit. It is especially useful for working with heart-centered stones like rose quartz and jade.

12. "The Green Witch: Your Complete Guide to the Natural Magic of Herbs, Flowers, Essential Oils, and More" by Arin Murphy-Hiscock

- **Overview:** An exploration of the natural magic found in plants, flowers, oils, and other elements. The book provides instructions for creating herbal remedies, potions, teas, and rituals.
- **Why It's Recommended:** This guide aligns perfectly with Libra's love for nature and beauty. It provides in-depth knowledge of herbs like rose, chamomile, and lavender, explaining how to use them in spells and rituals for love, peace, and emotional balance.

Section 5: Advanced Astrology

13. "Parker's Astrology: The Definitive Guide to Using Astrology in Every Aspect of Your Life" by Julia and Derek Parker

- **Overview:** An in-depth resource that covers all aspects of astrology, including planets, houses, aspects, and chart interpretation. This book provides detailed instructions for casting and analyzing a natal chart.
- **Why It's Recommended:** This book is ideal for Libras ready to delve into advanced astrology, offering tools to understand the intricate interplay of celestial energies. Its detailed content helps in interpreting the influence of Venus and other planetary movements on Libra's life and spellcasting.

14. "Planets in Transit: Life Cycles for Living" by Robert Hand

- **Overview:** A comprehensive guide to planetary transits and how they affect individual lives. The book explains the influence of each planet as it moves through the zodiac signs and aspects natal planets.

- **Why It's Recommended:** This book offers advanced insight into how planetary transits, such as Venus transiting through Libra, impact emotions, relationships, and spellwork. It's a valuable resource for timing rituals and understanding the ebb and flow of Libran energy.

15. "Astrology and the Authentic Self: Integrating Traditional and Modern Astrology to Uncover the Essence of the Birth Chart" by Demetra George

- **Overview:** This book merges traditional and modern astrological techniques to provide a holistic approach to chart interpretation. It emphasizes self-awareness and personal growth through astrology.
- **Why It's Recommended:** For Libras interested in exploring their deeper self and achieving inner harmony, this book offers a nuanced perspective on how various astrological components shape their personality and spiritual journey.

Final Thoughts on Book Recommendations

The books listed in this appendix cater to a range of interests and expertise levels, from astrology basics to advanced spellcraft and crystal work. Whether you're beginning your journey or expanding your magical practice, these resources provide detailed guidance on how to harness Libra's energies, work with Venus, and create rituals that align with your desire for harmony and beauty. By exploring these texts, you can deepen your understanding of astrology and spellcraft, empowering you to live in balance and achieve your fullest potential as a Libra.

<u>Message from the Author:</u>

I hope you enjoyed this book, I love astrology and knew there was not a book such as this out on the shelf. I love metaphysical items as well. Please check out my other books:

-Life of Government Benefits

-My life of Hell

-My life with Hydrocephalus

-Red Sky

-World Domination:Woman's rule

-World Domination:Woman's Rule 2: The War

-Life and Banishment of Apophis: book 1

-The Kidney Friendly Diet

-The Ultimate Hemp Cookbook

-Creating a Dispensary(legally)

-Cleanliness throughout life: the importance of showering from childhood to adulthood.

-Strong Roots: The Risks of Overcoddling children

-Hemp Horoscopes: Cosmic Insights and Earthly Healing

- Celestial Hemp Navigating the Zodiac: Through the Green Cosmos

-Astrological Hemp: Aligning The Stars with Earth's Ancient Herb

-The Astrological Guide to Hemp: Stars, Signs, and Sacred Leaves

-Green Growth: Innovative Marketing Strategies for your Hemp Products and Dispensary

-Cosmic Cannabis

-Astrological Munchies

-Henry The Hemp

-Zodiacal Roots: The Astrological Soul Of Hemp

- **Green Constellations: Intersection of Hemp and Zodiac**

-Hemp in The Houses: An astrological Adventure Through The Cannabis Galaxy

-Galactic Ganja Guide

Heavenly Hemp

Zodiac Leaves

Doctor Who Astrology

Cannastrology

Stellar Satvias and Cosmic Indicas

Celestial Cannabis: A Zodiac Journey

AstroHerbology: The Sky and The Soil: Volume 1

AstroHerbology:Celestial Cannabis:Volume 2

Cosmic Cannabis Cultivation

The Starry Guide to Herbal Harmony: Volume 1

The Starry Guide to Herbal Harmony: Cannabis Universe: Volume 2

Yugioh Astrology: Astrological Guide to Deck, Duels and more

Nightmare Mansion: Echoes of The Abyss

Nightmare Mansion 2: Legacy of Shadows

Nightmare Mansion 3: Shadows of the Forgotten

Nightmare Mansion 4: Echoes of the Damned

The Life and Banishment of Apophis: Book 2

Nightmare Mansion: Halls of Despair

Healing with Herb: Cannabis and Hydrocephalus

Planetary Pot: Aligning with Astrological Herbs: Volume 1

Fast Track to Freedom: 30 Days to Financial Independence Using AI, Assets, and Agile Hustles

Cosmic Hemp Pathways

How to Become Financially Free in 30 Days: 10,000 Paths to Prosperity

Zodiacal Herbage: Astrological Insights: Volume 1

Nightmare Mansion: Whispers in the Walls

The Daleks Invade Atlantis

Henry the hemp and Hydrocephalus

10X The Kidney Friendly Diet

Cannabis Universe: Adult coloring book

Hemp Astrology: The Healing Power of the Stars

Zodiacal Herbage: Astrological Insights: Cannabis Universe: Volume 2

Planetary Pot: Aligning with Astrological Herbs: Cannabis Universes: Volume 2

Doctor Who Meets the Replicators and SG-1: The Ultimate Battle for Survival

Nightmare Mansion: Curse of the Blood Moon

The Celestial Stoner: A Guide to the Zodiac

Cosmic Pleasures: Sex Toy Astrology for Every Sign

Hydrocephalus Astrology: Navigating the Stars and Healing Waters

Lapis and the Mischievous Chocolate Bar

Celestial Positions: Sexual Astrology for Every Sign

Apophis's Shadow Work Journal: : A Journey of Self-Discovery and Healing

Kinky Cosmos: Sexual Kink Astrology for Every Sign

Digital Cosmos: The Astrological Diginum Cumpendium

Stellar Seeds: The Cosmic Guide to Growing with Astrology

Apophis's Daily Gratitude Journal

Cat Astrology: Feline Mysteries of the Cosmos

The Cosmic Kama Sutra: An Astrological Guide to Sexual Positions

Unleash Your Potential: A Guided Journal Powered by AI Insights

Whispers of the Enchanted Grove

Cosmic Pleasures: An Astrological Guide to Sexual Kinks

369, 12 Manifestation Journal

Whisper of the nocturne journal(blank journal for writing or drawing)

The Boogey Book

Locked In Reflection: A Chastity Journey Through Locktober

Generating Wealth Quickly:

How to Generate $100,000 in 24 Hours

Star Magic: Harness the Power of the Universe

The Flatulence Chronicles: A Fart Journal for Self-Discovery

The Doctor and The Death Moth

Seize the Day: A Personal Seizure Tracking Journal

The Ultimate Boogeyman Safari: A Journey into the Boogie World and Beyond

Whispers of Samhain: 1,000 Spells of Love, Luck, and Lunar Magic: Samhain Spell Book

Apophis's guides:

Witch's Spellbook Crafting Guide for Halloween

Frost & Flame: The Enchanted Yule Grimoire of 1000 Winter Spells

The Ultimate Boogey Goo Guide & Spooky Activities for Halloween Fun

If you want solar for your home go here: https://www.harborsolar.live/apophisenterprises/

Get Some Tarot cards: https://www.makeplayingcards.com/sell/apophis-occult-shop

Get some shirts: https://www.bonfire.com/store/apophis-shirt-emporium/

Instagrams:
@apophis_enterprises,
@apophisbookemporium,
@apophisscardshop
Twitter: @apophisenterpr1
 Tiktok:@apophisenterprise
Youtube: @sg1fan23477, @FiresideRetreatKingdom

Podcast: Apophis Chat Zone: https://open.spotify.com/show/ 5zXbrCLEV2xzCp8ybrfHsk?si=fb4d4fdbdce44dec

Newsletter: https://apophiss-newsletter-27c897.beehiiv.com/

Milton Keynes UK
Ingram Content Group UK Ltd.
UKHW032037191024
449814UK00011B/682